Converting Basements, Garages & Attics

Converting Basements, Garages & Attics

Expanding Your Usable Space Easily, Attractively & Affordably

R. Dodge Woodson

 Sterling Publishing Co., Inc. New York

Library of Congress Cataloging-in-Publication Data

Woodson, R. Dodge (Roger Dodge), 1955–
    Converting basements, garages & attics : expanding your usable
space easily, attractively & affordably / by R. Dodge Woodson.
      p.   cm.
    Includes index.
    ISBN 0-8069-8740-5
    1. Dwellings—Remodeling—Amateurs' manuals. I. Title.
II. Title: Converting basements, garages, and attics.
TH4816.W627   1993
643'.7—dc20   92-37688
                                              CIP

10 9 8 7 6 5 4 3 2 1

Published in 1993 by Sterling Publishing Company, Inc.
387 Park Avenue South, New York, N.Y. 10016
© 1993 by R. Dodge Woodson
Distributed in Canada by Sterling Publishing
% Canadian Manda Group, P.O. Box 920, Station U
Toronto, Ontario, Canada M8Z 5P9
Distributed in Great Britain and Europe by Cassell PLC
Villiers House, 41/47 Strand, London WC2N 5JE, England
Distributed in Australia by Capricorn Link Ltd.
P.O. Box 665, Lane Cove, NSW 2066
Manufactured in the United Sates of America
All rights reserved

Sterling ISBN 0-8069-8740-5

Metric Equivalents

INCHES TO MILLIMETRES AND CENTIMETRES

MM—millimetres   CM—centimetres

Inches	MM	CM	Inches	CM	Inches	CM
⅛	3	0.3	9	22.9	30	76.2
¼	6	0.6	10	25.4	31	78.7
⅜	10	1.0	11	27.9	32	81.3
½	13	1.3	12	30.5	33	83.8
⅝	16	1.6	13	33.0	34	86.4
¾	19	1.9	14	35.6	35	88.9
⅞	22	2.2	15	38.1	36	91.4
1	25	2.5	16	40.6	37	94.0
1¼	32	3.2	17	43.2	38	96.5
1½	38	3.8	18	45.7	39	99.1
1¾	44	4.4	19	48.3	40	101.6
2	51	5.1	20	50.8	41	104.1
2½	64	6.4	21	53.3	42	106.7
3	76	7.6	22	55.9	43	109.2
3½	89	8.9	23	58.4	44	111.8
4	102	10.2	24	61.0	45	114.3
4½	114	11.4	25	63.5	46	116.8
5	127	12.7	26	66.0	47	119.4
6	152	15.2	27	68.6	48	121.9
7	178	17.8	28	71.1	49	124.5
8	203	20.3	29	73.7	50	127.0

Contents

The first color section follows page 32.

The second color section follows page 64.

The third color section follows page 96.

The fourth color section follows page 128.

The fifth color section follows page 160.

Introduction

Remodelling can be full of fun and adventure, but it can also harbor disappointment. This book will help you overcome the fear of remodelling. By converting your basement, attic, or garage to living space, you can add value to your home. This book will show you how to make successful conversions—by doing it yourself.

Acting as your own general contractor may reduce your remodelling costs by twenty percent or more. If you do your own plumbing, you can save even more. The more you do yourself, the more money you'll save. While you're saving money, you'll be building equity in your home.

I'm a custom remodeller and a general contractor, with eighteen years of experience in the building trades. Learning from my mistakes and my experience, you'll avoid costly errors, and you'll enjoy your remodelling experience.

As you read this book, you'll find hundreds of illustrations, detailing various aspects of your job, and showing what type of fabulous results you can achieve. The photographs will give you ideas for and examples of all types of conversion project.

This book begins with assessing your present conditions. Then you'll read about plans, material take-offs, and estimates. Before you actually begin remodelling, you'll see how to make the most of your existing space.

Chapter 4 will show you full-blown conversion techniques. You'll begin by raising the roof and then move on to cover almost all aspects of attic, basement, and garage conversions.

Building a dormer is described in chapter 9. Rough-plumbing pointers are found in chapter 11. Facts on floor coverings can be found in chapter 17, and chapter 19 will show you how to clean your new fixtures, floors, and more.

1
Assessing Present Conditions

Before you begin your conversion, assess present conditions. Attics, basements, and garages all offer desirable possibilities for conversion into living space. The attic that has never been used for anything more than storage can become a handsome study, or it can provide space for extra bedrooms. Your dingy, grey basement can be transformed into a glowing entertainment room. Garages can be converted to provide independent living for teenagers and in-laws.

The ordinary homeowner can convert these spaces, with the exception of some aspects of the job, like complicated electrical or plumbing work. The first step in the conversion process is to determine what there is to work with. To minimize expenses and maximize usable space, you must do some planning.

This chapter will answer many of the questions most often asked of professional remodellers and this chapter will also ask *you* questions. These latter questions are meant to make you think and to analyze your personal circumstances.

Basements

Many houses have basements. A basement may be either a walk-out basement, a daylight basement, or a buried basement. A walk-out basement is a basement that has its own outside entrance. The entrance to a walk-out basement is either a standard entry door or a patio-type door. The door to a walk-out basement should open at ground level. Basements that have bulkhead doors are not considered walk-out basements. Walk-out basements offer the most conversion options.

A daylight basement is a basement with full-size windows in the basement walls. Daylight basements may also be walk-out basements, but frequently they aren't. Daylight basements are often found in split-foyer homes. These basements are good candidates for conversion.

Buried basements are those with all their walls surrounded by earth. The only windows in buried basements are small foundation windows. Incoming natural light is limited in this type of basement. A buried basement is the least desirable candidate for conversion.

Assessing Buried Basements

The first step in assessing your basement conversion is to determine your goals. Buried basements are limited in their uses, but they can be ideal playrooms for children, or entertainment rooms for adults.

If you're considering converting a buried basement into an additional bedroom, you may be out of luck. Most building codes require bedrooms to have a means of emergency egress. This code requirement ensures the safety of the bedroom's occupant in case of fire. The "egress rule" is usually fulfilled by the placement of large windows. The exact size of egress windows required may vary from code to code, but most codes have *some* rules for emergency egress.

Since buried basements don't allow for the installation of egress windows, converting this type of basement into bedrooms is not likely to meet local building-code requirements. This is just one example of how building codes may prevent certain conversions. Before you begin any conversion, check with local code-enforcement authorities to determine what it is that you need to comply with local codes.

Moisture is common in buried basements. Since buried basements don't receive the same amount of ventilation as above-ground living space, mould, mildew, and even standing water can all be problems. These problems can be overcome, but you must determine if they are present before you begin your conversion.

Many basements contain columns that support the floor above the basement. These columns can reduce the effectiveness of converted basement space. For example, putting a billiard table in the basement is a fine idea, but if the columns get in your way, your conversion will never live up to your dreams. Don't despair; these columns can be removed.

Does your basement have pipes or ducts that hang below the floor joists? Unfinished basements are known for this type of obstacle. Will you need more height than what will result from dropping the ceiling to conceal these pipes and ducts? In most cases, these overhead obstructions can be relocated.

Are you considering installing a bathroom in your basement? When a basement is converted to living space, adding a bathroom enhances its utility. However, many basements don't have plumbing under the floor. It's not uncommon for the main plumbing to be located *above* the basement floor. Standard plumbing installation is impossible under such conditions.

When the building drain is located *above* the basement floor, you must use specialized plumbing techniques, typically involving the installation of a sewer sump and a pump. While not particularly difficult to install, this type of plumbing can add hundreds of dollars to the cost of adding a bathroom.

Assessing Daylight Basements

Daylight basements offer more conversion options than do buried basements. Daylight basements are also better places (than are buried basements) to invest your money. Converting a basement to living space is one of the least expensive ways to gain usable space, but it isn't always the most cost-effective way. A full-scale conversion of a buried basement may not result in a full return on investment. The same conversion of a daylight basement or a walk-out basement may balance return on investment.

Daylight basements present nearly unlimited conversion options. These basements may still be subject to moisture problems, but these problems are not likely to be as extensive as they could be with buried basements. Since daylight basements are partially above ground, adding bedrooms is a real option. With these basements, the installation of egress windows is possible.

Most builders assume that daylight basements may be converted to living space at some future date, so builders generally are careful about the placement of mechanical equipment, columns, pipes, and ducts. You may even find that you have, in your daylight basement, plumbing roughed in for a future bathroom.

Walk-Out Basements

Walk-out basements offer the most options for conversion of all basement styles. Since a walk-out basement has its own independent outside access, the basement can be converted to meet almost any need. Walk-out basements are often used as private sanctuaries for teenagers or to accommodate in-laws. Although basement conversion is not generally the best way to build equity in your home, converting a walk-out basement *is* usually a *safe* way.

Attics

When you need more space, your attic is a great place to look for it. Of course, some attics offer better conversion potential than do others, but attics, in general, are good candidates for conversion.

Attics make it possible for handy homeowners to build equity in their homes. While basement conversions rarely add more value to a home than what they cost, attic conversions can be worth much more than what they cost. If you're looking for a conversion project with profit potential, look to your attic.

Attic conversions can be either fairly simple or quite complicated. The skills required for an attic conversion can be more demanding than those needed for a basement conversion. The extent of the skills required will be determined by the type of attic you are starting with and the extent of the changes you plan to make.

Attic Considerations

Many factors must be considered in attic conversions. Since your attic was built as an attic, it may need some structural improvements before it can accommodate living space. You may have to increase the size of the joists, or it may be necessary to add a dormer to obtain satisfactory ceiling height. The insulation in your attic may have to be moved or replaced.

How will you get to your new attic living space? Will you be able to use a conventional staircase, or will you have to use a spiral stairway? If you'll be installing plumbing in your attic, how will you route the plumbing through the existing finished walls below? These are only a few of the considerations you must look at before you begin your attic conversion.

Garages

Garages can provide extensive living space, and at reasonable cost. You might use just the lower level of the garage, or you could expand into the attic of the garage. If your garage isn't already attached to your home, add a breezeway to increase its usability. Like walk-out basements, garages offer ideal living arrangements for semi-independent teenagers and for in-laws.

The right garage conversion can add equity to your property. With the right ideas and circumstances, you can make the garage a part of your home. By using some simple exterior-design applications, you can dress the garage up to be a handsome addition to the house. When these methods are used, equity gains can soar.

Even when you're unwilling to give up the convenience of garaging your car, you can convert the garage attic into a studio or other living space. There's potential for great garage conversions.

Garage conversions are relatively simple. The structure is already framed. The roof, siding, and floor are all in place. With such a good head start, converting a garage appeals to many homeowners. The effect of garage conversion on the appraised value of your home will depend on how the conversion is done and the placement of your garage, but the odds are good that you won't *lose* money.

Ask a Professional

The section that follows will answer some questions homeowners most often ask professionals.

Common Questions About Basements

During the rainy season my basement leaks. Is there anything I can do to prevent this?

Yes. You can install a perimeter drain around the exterior walls of the your basement. This is most often done inside the basement. The installation requires breaking the concrete floor (usually with a rented jackhammer) and digging a trench around the walls. Then, a perimeter drain is placed in the trench. The perimeter drain, a slotted pipe buried in crushed stone, conveys invading water to a sump. A sump pump removes the water from the sump.

My basement is always musty. What can I do about it?

Dehumidifiers often work wonders on damp and musty basements. Adding ventilation to the basement will also help.

I have a buried basement with a bulkhead door. I want to install a normal entry door; can this be done?

Yes. You can remove the bulkhead door and use the foundation (where the bulkhead door was originally mounted) to frame an entryway. This type of installation usually involves building a small gable roof that attaches to the house, and framing walls to accept the normal entry door.

I have support columns in my basement that inhibit my remodelling plans. Is there anything that can be done about them?

Yes. By adding a flitch plate or an I-beam, the columns can be removed.

I'm converting my basement into finished living space, and I want to hide my mechanical equipment in a closet. Will that be O.K.?

It all depends upon the type of equipment you'd be enclosing. Some mechanical equipment needs air circulation to operate properly. Other equipment needs minimum clearance from combustible materials. Before placing a tight enclosure around mechanical equipment, have an expert evaluate the machinery and the configuration for clearance and ventilation requirements.

I'm planning to convert my basement into living space. Do I need any permits or code inspections for this type of work?

Depending upon the extent of your work, you may need to obtain permits and have your work inspected. Almost any alteration to plumbing, heating, and electrical systems will require permits and inspections. Building inspections may also be required.

Common Questions About Attics

I'm converting my attic into living space, and I want to tie my new bathroom into the big pipe that runs up through my attic. Will this be all right?

The big pipe you're referring to is the home's main vent. Many of these vents can be converted to stack vents to accept drainage, but you should check with a licensed plumber to be sure.

I need to get hot- and cold-water pipes up into my attic. How can I do it?

Many remodellers bring pipes up into an attic through closets or other natural chases in the house. In some cases, it's possible to drill the top and bottom plates of a partition and to snake the pipes up into the attic. Another option is to open one of the lower finished partitions to allow the plumbing installation. However, such an opening may require extensive repairs.

I'm converting my attic into living space. It has 2"×8" joists; will these be strong enough to accommodate the new use?

Not necessarily. The size of the floor joists to use is determined by span and weight load. There is a good chance that the 2"×8" joists will be adequate, but you must check with local code requirements to be sure and also to be safe.

I have an old boiler that provides heat to my home. Will it be big enough to heat the new space I create with my attic conversion?

Heating systems are rated by BTU ratings. Before you can determine if an existing heating system can handle additional demands, you must arrive at heat-loss figures. Most utility companies provide such a service to their customers, often without cost.

I'm just going to finish my attic into living space. I don't need fancy blueprints, do I?

You probably won't need "high-tech" blueprints, but your town's code-enforcement office is likely to require some plans and specifications.

Common Questions About Garages

I want to add living space over my garage, but the garage roof is held up by engineered trusses. Do they have to be replaced?

There are three types of truss: roof trusses, attic-storage trusses, and room trusses. If you have room trusses, you probably won't have to replace them, but if you have roof or attic-storage trusses, some additional structural strength will be needed. However, this doesn't mean you have to replace your trusses; you may be able to simply add new structural members to the support system.

I'm converting my garage to living space, and I already have electricity in my garage. Can I connect to the existing electrical system for the rest of my conversion?

It's unlikely. You don't want to overload electrical circuits. Consult a licensed electrician, but expect to add new circuits.

I want to install carpet on the floor of my garage, but I'm afraid it will be damaged by moisture. Is there anything I can do?

Yes. You can build a "sleeper system" of floor joists and then install a wooden subfloor. This means installing pressure-treated lumber on the concrete floor (as floor joists), and then attaching a standard plywood subfloor to the sleeper-joist system. This construction will reduce the effects of moisture and will provide a warm and soft floor.

2
Making Plans, Material Take-Offs & Estimates

Proper planning is an essential element in a successful remodelling project. Without good planning you could exceed your budget, or your job could lack appeal. This chapter will teach you how to make plans, material take-offs, and estimates. While these aspects of your remodelling job don't require a hammer and nails, they're still important.

General Planning

General planning can involve anything from the choice of paint color you'll use to how much you can afford to spend on the job.

Assume for a moment that you're converting the upstairs of your garage to a bedroom. Your garage is 24′ × 24′, and it's attached to your house.

How high should the ceiling be?

An 8′ ceiling height is standard, but you could get by with a ceiling height of 7′6″. Any ceiling height lower than 7′6″ probably won't pass local building codes, and such a low ceiling would have a detrimental effect on your property's appraised value.

Will I have to alter the pitch of the existing garage roof to obtain a satisfactory ceiling height?

There's a good chance that you will. You can make this determination by measuring from the bottom of the ceiling joists in your garage to the finished floor level of your home. Remember to allow for the thickness of the new ceiling and the new flooring in your converted space.

If I'm forced to alter the pitch on my garage roof, will the added pitch interfere with existing windows in my home?

As you increase the roof pitch, the roof will reach higher onto the side of your house. Altering the roof pitch may leave unsightly areas on your house's siding where the old roof attached to it.

How will I get new electrical wiring into the converted space? Will I be installing a bathroom in part of the space? How will I get the plumbing into the area above the garage? Will the house's existing drain and sewer handle the increased load of a new bathroom?

In most places, a 3″ building drain is not allowed to carry the waste from more than two toilets. Adding a third toilet could mean replacing your sewer or parts of your building drain.

As you can see, important questions are arising quickly. The planning stage of your project is no small task. If you do your planning properly, it will save you time and money. If you do it wrong, you will regret it for years to come.

Your general planning requirements will vary, depending on the nature of your project. One good way of planning is to work with a checklist.

Your checklist should have a spot for every phase of work you anticipate doing. As you plan, check off the items you've already covered. Have professionals come in to give you bids and advice. Even if you do the work yourself, the pros may point out things you've neglected.

Keep resale value in mind when you plan your conversion. A feature you love may not be appreciated by future home buyers and appraisers. Avoid functional obsolescence. For example, if the only access to a new attic living space is a spiral stairway, how will you get furniture up there? While spiral stairs add a touch of flair and are a reasonable second means of access, they aren't the preferred means of access.

Most people's dreams are restricted by the reality of their budgets. Grandiose plans are fine, but when the time comes to pay for them, the dream may turn into a nightmare. The best way to avoid overspending is to obtain *firm* estimates on all your expenditures, including the "hidden" expenses. To get such estimates, you need plans and material "take-offs."

Drawing Floor Plans

Drawing floor plans doesn't always require an architect. You may be able to draw your own plans for small jobs. In some cases, a draftsperson or even your local lumber supplier may be able to produce the plans. The important thing is to have a set of working plans.

If you're just finishing a basement but not affecting the structural integrity of your home, you should be able to draw your own plans (Illus. 2-1). Converting your garage may also be possible using home-drawn plans. But, when it comes to adding dormers and performing major structural work, consult a professional.

For small jobs, a simple line drawing may be the only plan you need. As the difficulty of the job escalates, so does the need for more detailed plans and specifications. Many lumber suppliers will provide you with detailed working plans when you buy your supplies from them. The cost for these plans is minimal. On the other hand, if you have an architect draw your blueprints, be prepared to spend a good deal of money.

Include in your working plans as much information as you can. The more detailed the plans, the fewer problems you'll have later. Blueprints use a number of symbols to represent building components. In order to read blueprints, you should understand what these symbols mean. I have included a number of illustrations to show the types of symbols that you might encounter on your working plans.

Cross sections and details are usually shown on working plans for major jobs. These detail sections can show such items as stairs or wall cut-throughs. A joist detail will show the placement, spacing, and size of floor joists. A truss detail will identify the type of truss to be used and pertinent information about the truss. I've also included some drawings to show you what these details might look like on your plans.

Material Take-Offs

Material take-offs are, simply, lists of materials you anticipate needing. These lists are typically made by reviewing the working plans and making a list of materials.

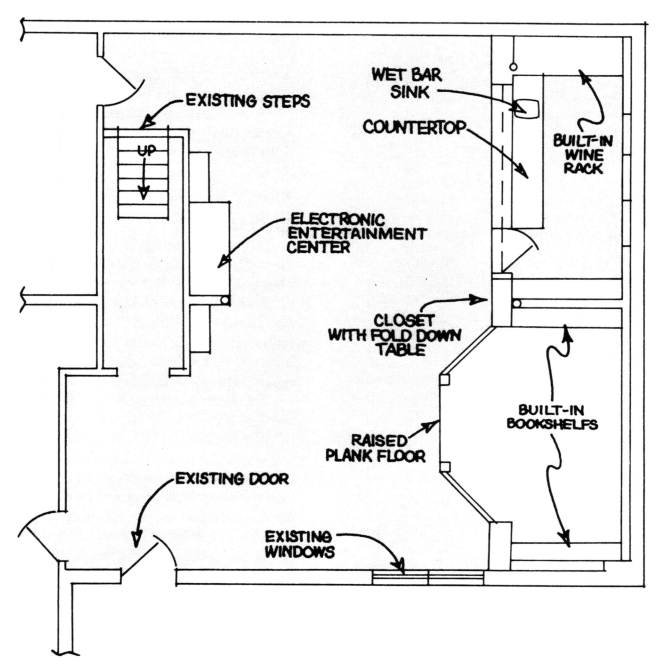

Illus. 2-1. Sample floor plan. Drawing courtesy of Georgia-Pacific Corp.

Most of those not accustomed to making take-offs will leave out many needed components. For example, the average person would probably not figure the amount of "dead wood" needed to frame a dormer. Nails are often overlooked, as are adhesives and similar less apparent needs. These small items can add up to a substantial sum.

One way to develop a material list is to ask your lumber supplier to do it for you. Most suppliers are willing to provide material lists from your plans, but the quality of their lists may leave something to be desired. Two factors work against you under these circumstances.

Some suppliers will casually forget a few

items, making their price quotes more attractive. Even well-meaning suppliers are likely to be in a rush and miss some items you'll need. Since the supplier is not usually being paid to develop a material list, the quality of his list may not be the best.

If you're having your plans drawn by an architect or a drafting firm, you may be able to arrange for these people to create an accurate take-off. Since they will be paid and won't have a stake in your purchase of material, they're more likely than a supplier would be to make up an unbiased and accurate list.

The best way to arrive at an accurate material take-off (if you have the ability) is to do it yourself. Depending upon the quality of your plans, this may not be such a demanding task. Many blueprints go into great detail. They show joist diagrams and headers. They show electrical boxes and wiring routes. If you have such detailed plans, making a good take-off won't be difficult.

If you compile your own material list, you'll benefit from some of these pointers. Pick a set of plans to be used for the primary purpose of doing a take-off. Use a checklist to reduce the likelihood of missed items. As you count items, circle them with a red pencil. This will help you to avoid duplication, and it will make it easy to see if you have forgotten anything. When you think you've calculated all of your materials, add a percentage of materials for waste and mistakes. By adding a percentage (say 5%) to your lumber list, you make it unlikely you'll run short of material or money.

An ideal way to come up with the most accurate take-off is to combine methods. First, do your own take-off. Then have your building supplier do a take-off. If feasible, have the person who drew the plans also generate a material list. Then, compare all of the lists and look for discrepancies.

After comparing all of your lists and noting all of the differences, investigate to see which lists are right and which ones are incorrect. By using this comparative method you ensure accuracy.

Estimates

The next step is to obtain estimates for all labor and material to be used in your job. If you're doing all of the work yourself, the labor cost may not be important to you, but you still might want to look at the time you'll be spending on different phases of the work.

Just as an example: I've never found a way to install insulation that was more cost-effective than to subcontract that job to an insulation contractor.

By looking at how much time you'll spend on certain phases of your job, you may discover that your time may be better spent by following some other pursuit.

Material Prices

Once you have an accurate take-off, getting price quotes for material will be easy. All you have to do is circulate your material list among suppliers and request a *formal quote*. Note that I said a *formal quote*, not an *estimate*. Most material suppliers will quote prices that are good for at least thirty days. Get the quotes in writing and compare them closely.

The "bottom-line" (cheapest) figure can be deceiving. If the supplier has omitted items or substituted items, the price quoted will not be a fair comparison with the prices from other bidders. Check each quote, item by item, to be sure that they are competitive bids.

Labor Prices

Labor prices, if you need to obtain them, are more difficult to compare. It's easy to get three bids from three different plumbers, but not all plumbers are the same. There are some key issues to consider when you decide to use a subcontractor.

Insurance is a major issue. A contractor without adequate insurance is a strong liability to you. What happens if an electrician burns down your house or if a plumber floods it? If these contractors aren't insured, where will the money for repairs come from? All contractors should have basic liability insurance. If the contractor has employees, workers' compensation insurance is normally required. You can confirm a contractor's insurance coverage by asking him for a certificate of insurance. If you request these certificates, they should come to you through the mail from the insurance company, not from the contractor.

Once you're satisfied that the contractors bidding for your work are reputable, stable, and properly insured, you have much of the battle won. However, it still isn't easy to compare bids for labor. Beware of contractors who give you hourly rates for doing the job. It's almost always best to get a firm price for the full contract. When you allow a contractor to work at an hourly rate, the costs can get out of hand. By working with written contracts, you can control costs.

One of the most difficult chores when comparing contractors is comparing the quality of their work. Try to arrange to see finished examples of each contractor's work. The process of choosing the best contractors can be time-consuming and frustrating, but cutting corners on your research can have disastrous results.

Hidden Costs

Hidden costs can sneak up on you. Have you included the cost of your building, plumbing, electrical, and heating permits? Have you included a price for trash removal? If you're financing your job, have you calculated the fees associated with the loan, such as appraisals, title searches, and the like? Depending upon the nature of your job, these hidden expenses can mount.

Putting It All Together

Once you have your plans, take-offs, and estimates, all that's left is to put it all together. Take a second look at your plans, and you may find subtle changes you want to make. Now's the time to make them, for making changes during the job can be very costly.

If you've compared your take-offs thoroughly, you should feel confident about your material needs. Your estimates, or (better yet) quotes, will give you some comfort in the cost of your endeavor, but don't be lulled into a false sense of security with your pricing information.

Labor and material prices do fluctuate. If your job is postponed or delayed, prices may change. It's also conceivable that certain materials or contractors won't be available when you need them. If this happens, you may have to go to your second choice of material or contractor. Going to the second choice often means spending more money.

If you've planned well, there won't be many unexpected costs. Even so, you should allow yourself a margin of error. Some contractors use a 5% "float factor" and others use a "slush pile" of 10%. Allow at least this much, and probably more, to be sure you don't exceed your budget.

3
Using Existing Space

Making good use of existing space can save you money and enhance your remodelling project. Too many people, homeowners and contractors alike, fail to recognize the value and benefits of using existing space. This chapter presents ideas to consider when using existing space.

Almost any project will provide the opportunity to use existing space. When you begin to plan, take a close look at any existing features or space that you can incorporate into your job.

Go through the area to be remodelled and note what you see. Wait a few days and then repeat your inspection of the space. See if you notice anything that you didn't see on your first walk-through. If you've lived in your home a long time, there may be many features that you have come to take for granted.

It may be easier for an outside contractor to determine how to use existing space, first, because he doesn't live in your home and can be more objective than you can, and, second, because of the experience a professional contractor has. With these two factors combined, it's easy for a contractor to see aspects of your job that elude you. Each job will present its own set of problems and advantages.

Buried Basements

Buried basements may offer the fewest options for using existing features and space. These basements, in their unfinished state, have few amenities. What should you look for in an unfinished buried basement?

Outside Entrance

Not all buried basements have any outside entrance, but many do have a bulkhead door. If your basement has an outside entrance, capitalize on its location by framing a small entryway and adding a full-size entrance door to increase the basement's usability. If you have a wood stove in your basement, this outside doorway can make wood handling much easier. Having a standard entry will encourage more use of the basement's independent access. In addition to the convenience, a new door can provide an emergency exit.

Some bulkhead doors leak. If you're finishing your basement, the last thing you want is a door that leaks. By building a stand-up entry, you eliminate the possibility of water leaking around the bulkhead.

Stairs

The stairs going into your basement can probably be used in your conversion. Depending upon your new design, it may be necessary to alter the existing stairs to include a winder or similar change in direction, but the existing stairs can normally be used.

The Floor

Your existing basement floor can be used. Many people feel a need to spend large amounts of money to alter the basement floor. If you're fortunate enough to have a consistently dry basement, there's no need to build a sleeper system for a new floor. There are carpets and pads available that will work well on concrete floors. These materials are typically meant for use in commercial buildings, but they're attractive and they'll work well in your home. There are also vinyl floor coverings that will do a good job on a basement floor.

Depending upon the degree of finishing you are doing, you may be able to get by simply by sealing and painting the concrete floor. This finish will reduce moisture and dust problems.

Floor Drains and Plumbing Stacks

Floor drains and plumbing stacks that extend beneath your basement floor are a good place to start when adding a basement bath. The local plumbing code will set limits on what you can add to existing pipes, but in many cases you can add fixtures to existing plumbing. Even if you don't have plumbing below your basement floor, look for existing piping. If you are forced to pump your waste water up, it will help to keep the pump as close to a gravity drain as possible.

Mechanical Equipment

Most basements contain mechanical equipment, such as furnaces and water heaters. Good builders try to group these items near each other, but some contractors put them wherever it's convenient. Assess the locations of such mechanical equipment.

Heating systems are usually the most difficult equipment to relocate. Water heaters can normally be moved without great expense. Houses with wells will have water storage (pressure) tanks that can also be relocated without a major investment. Depending upon your space needs, you might find it is beneficial to relocate mechanical equipment to a central location.

Electrical Wiring

Most basements are equipped with a minimum amount of electrical wiring. But, you'll be able to use the existing light boxes and receptacles. Look for the main electrical box. Newer homes will have a circuit-breaker box; older homes will have a fuse box. The area in front of the electrical panel must be left accessible. This accessibility could alter your plans.

Daylight Basements

Daylight basements are similar to buried basements when you evaluate their remodelling potential. The big difference between the two is the windows that are found in daylight basements. If you're planning to convert your basement into sleeping space, remember the need for a means of emergency exit. The windows, if they're large enough, can provide this, but even if they aren't, it will be easier to replace existing windows with larger ones than it would be to cut in new window openings.

Walk-Out Basements

Walk-out basements have the big advantage of a ground-level entry. Real-estate appraisers are much more generous appraising a finished walk-out basement than they are appraising a finished buried basement. The value of converting a daylight basement falls between that of converting a buried basement and that of converting a walk-out basement. If you have a walk-out basement, it's possible to have its value reach a point equal to, or near, the value of the other extra living space in your home. For example, a finished walk-out basement may have a value of $25.00 per square foot. In comparison, a finished buried basement may only have a value of $10.00 per square foot. Of course, these figures may vary from region to region, but the concept remains the same.

Attics

Your attic may have space and features that you can incorporate into your conversion plans. Some roof designs lend themselves to expansion better than do others. Some attics are equipped with stairs suitable for everyday use.

Insulation

Attic insulation usually comes in two forms: blown-in insulation or batt insulation. If your attic has batt insulation, you may be able to use the existing insulation in your conversion project. If you have blown-in insulation, you won't be able to reuse it.

If you have blown-in insulation in the floor of your attic, it should be removed prior to your conversion. Once your attic is converted to heated living space, you'll want heat from the lower floors to pass up and into the new living space.

When batt insulation is laid on attic floors it can usually be picked up and reinstalled in the new framing. When converting most attics, you'll need insulation in the new walls and in the new attic you create. The new attic may be small, created only by collar ties, but it will still need to be insulated. If you're installing your old insulation in wall cavities, it will probably be necessary to place a moisture barrier over the insulation. It is common to use unfaced insulation in attic ceilings, but insulation installed in the walls should have a vapor barrier. Add a

vapor barrier by stapling plastic over the insulation and stapling it to the wall studs.

Stairs

Some attics are equipped with nothing more than a scuttle hole for access. Others have disappearing, or pull-down, stairs. If you're lucky, your attic will have a traditional full-size stairway. These stairs are fairly common in Colonial-style houses and in Cape Cods with unfinished attics. If you have a solid set of traditional stairs, they may be suitable for access to your new space.

Ventilation

When you convert your attic to living space, you'll still need good ventilation for the new attic you create. If your home has a ridge vent, such ventilation is in place already. If you have gable vents, you may find that their placement interferes with your plans. Rectangular gable vents often must be removed to make space for windows in attic conversions. If you must remove rectangular gable vents, consider installing a ridge vent or a triangular gable vent. The triangular vents are placed high on the gable end and are out of the way of windows. If you have soffit vents, don't frame your conversion in a way that will eliminate the vents' effectiveness. Leave a space for air to circulate in.

Ceiling Joists

When you go into your attic, inspect the existing ceiling joists. The existing joists may be strong enough to allow the attic conversion without replacing or adding to them. However, in most cases, additional joists will be required. Your local building code will provide guidelines for the size of joists needed for your specific use.

Roof Design

Your existing roof design may allow you to create living space with minimum effort. A gambrel roof lends itself to conversion very nicely. Ceiling height is often one of the biggest obstacles to overcome in an attic conversion. If you have a roof with a low pitch, you may have to build dormers to obtain needed ceiling space.

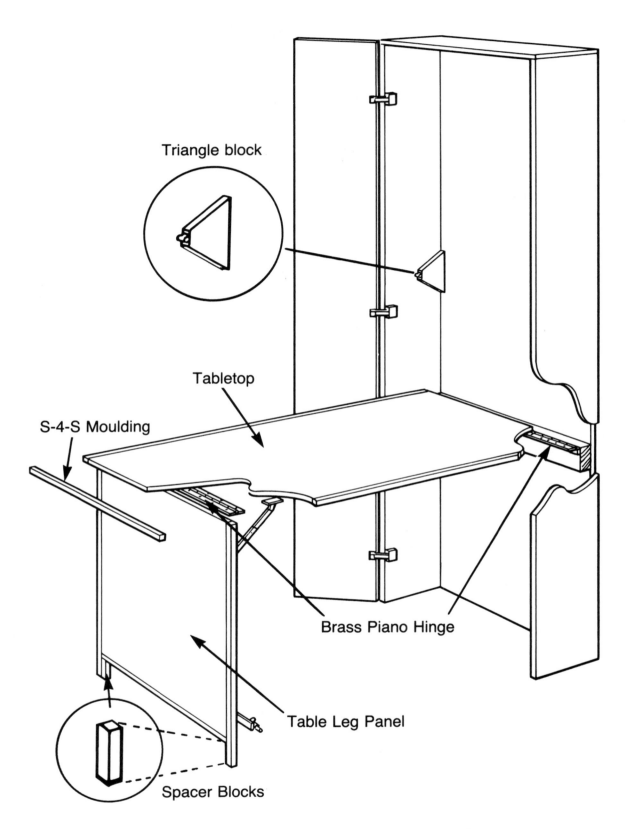

Triangle block

Tabletop

S-4-S Moulding

Brass Piano Hinge

Table Leg Panel

Spacer Blocks

Illus. 3-1. Drop-down table. Drawing courtesy of Georgia-Pacific Corp.

Garages

Garage conversions are generally much easier than attic conversions, since garages offer so many existing features and so much existing space to work with. Here are some of the benefits of a garage conversion.

Floor

Garages typically have concrete floors that can be used in the finished conversion. Some floors can be used as is, but others will need some special attention. If your garage is sloped to a central floor drain, it will be necessary to build a sleeper system of floor joists and to add a subfloor. If your floor is rough, such as the finish obtained by brushing the concrete, it may need to be smoothed out. This can be done by floating a filling compound over the floor. When your garage floor is level and smooth, it can be used as is.

Framing

With garage conversions, the framing of the structure is already done. All you have to do is add interior partitions and close in the opening where the large garage door is located.

Siding

The siding of your new structure is complete before you start your conversion.

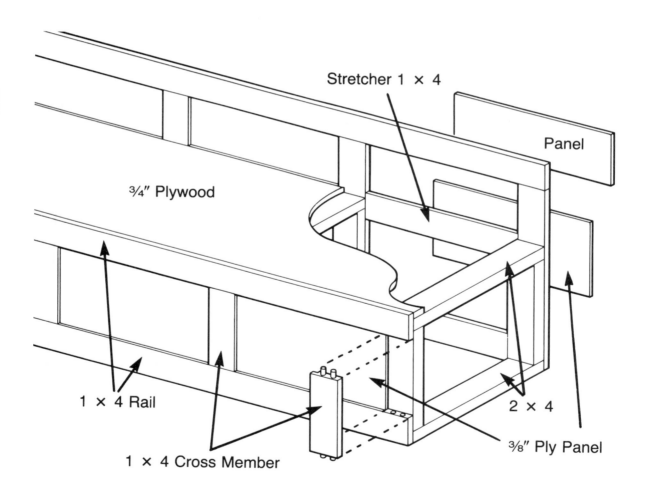

Illus. 3-2. Built-in bench seat. Drawing courtesy of Georgia-Pacific Corp.

Roofing

Your conversion is being done under an existing roof. In many cases the roof will not have to be altered. However, there are times when the roof structure and the roofing must be altered to increase the ceiling height in a two-story garage conversion.

Entry Door

Most garages have a standard three-foot entry door. With the proper design planning, you can use this door in its existing location.

Windows

Garage windows are not normally those that you would use in finished living space. You may be able to use existing windows, but you'll almost certainly have to add more.

Insulation

Garages are sometimes insulated. If your garage is insulated, you're one step closer to your finished conversion.

Drywall

Many garages have drywall on the interior walls and ceilings, another time- and money-saver.

Electrical Wiring

It's not uncommon for garages to already have electricity, but the electrical wiring is rarely enough to handle a full conversion. Expect to run new wiring to your garage conversion.

Getting a Head Start

By looking at what you already have, you'll be getting a head start on your conversion project. Any steps you can avoid and any materials you don't have to buy will save you time and money. You may also get ideas for built-in units, like drop-down tables or bench seats (Illus. 3-1 and Illus. 3-2).

4
Raising the Roof

If you plan to convert your attic (house or garage) into living space, you may have to raise the roof. This is an expensive and complicated procedure, but sometimes it's the only way to turn an attic into usable living space. Unless you're very handy and have some help available, this job is best left to professionals.

Why raise the roof? There are times when there simply isn't enough ceiling height to convert attic space into habitable space. Normally, a minimum ceiling height of 7'6" is required by building codes. As with any rule, there are exceptions. For example, it's often permissible to have a finished ceiling height of only 7' in a bathroom. Since many jurisdictions use different building codes and may interpret the codes differently, always check with the local building-code enforcement office before doing any major work.

Roof Trusses

Another reason why you may be forced to build a new roof is the presence of roof trusses in your existing roof. Roof trusses

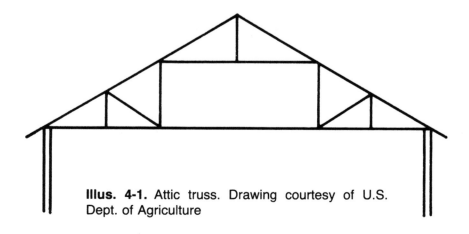

Illus. 4-1. Attic truss. Drawing courtesy of U.S. Dept. of Agriculture

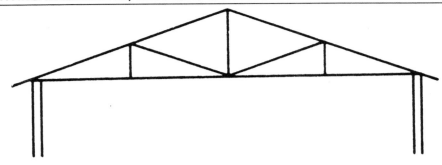

Illus. 4-2. Howe truss. Drawing courtesy of U.S. Dept. of Agriculture

are engineered to meet the requirements of their present use, not necessarily to meet the additional requirements of adding living space. Since trusses are engineered and built to exact standards, cutting or altering them can weaken or destroy their structural integrity.

Attic trusses (Illus. 4-1) and room trusses are two types of truss that you can work around to convert an attic to living space. These trusses are made with an open area in the middle of the truss. This opening allows freedom of movement between the trusses. While most trusses have pieces of wood weaving through them (Illus. 4-2) that prevent building a room, attic and room trusses don't have these pieces.

Even with attic trusses, some additional support will be required to convert the attic to living space. This extra support will normally require adding floor joists between the bottom plates of the trusses. Room trusses, on the other hand, are intended to be converted into living space. However, check the structural rating, and be sure that the rating is adequate for your proposed use.

Roof Pitch

The existing roof pitch may not allow you to convert your attic space. Roofs that have a low pitch offer a wide attic floor but a short ceiling height. A steep roof pitch provides

Illus. 4-3. Gambrel roof

Basement den. Photo courtesy of Georgia-Pacific Corp.

A

House before remodelling. Photo courtesy of Velux-America, Inc.

B

House after remodelling. Photo courtesy of Velux-America, Inc.

c

Kitchen design. Photo courtesy of Wood-Mode, Inc.

D

good headroom but makes for a narrow room.

Roof Design

Roof design can play a large role in the ease of attic conversions. The majority of American houses have gable roofs. Gable roofs are fine for attic expansion, but they often require the addition of dormers if a great deal of finished space is desired. A hip roof provides a good central height, but it lacks ceiling height around the exterior walls. Of the most common roof designs, the *gambrel* (Illus. 4-3) allows the most potential for expansion without the use of dormers.

The gambrel roof is the type of roof described throughout this chapter.

Trusses vs. Rafters

When you consider raising your roof, first look in your attic to see which type of roof system you presently have. If you have a stick-built roof system (one with rafters),

you should be able to salvage the existing joists. You may also be able to use much of the lumber from the old rafters. If you have any type of truss, other than attic or room trusses, they will have to be removed completely. This removal, of course, will mean substantial damage to the ceilings in the rooms below.

The ceilings in the room below will be attached to the joists in the attic floor. When you remove trusses, you are removing an entire unit of roof support and ceiling joists. However, a stick-built system will have independent rafters and ceiling joists. They will be nailed together, but they may be separated. In either case, you are likely to experience significant damage to the ceilings below.

Removing the Old Roof

If you decide to install a new roof, removing the old roof will be your first priority. This, obviously, is a big job. Before you begin ripping off the old roof, consider the following factors.

Illus. 4-4. Bottom cord of a truss

Rain

What will you do if it rains before you get the new roof on? This is a problem even for professionals. Many professionals will work the roof in sections. They will remove and rebuild *sections* of the roof, rather than stripping off the whole roof and trying to replace it before rain comes. At night, pros often cover the unprotected roof sections with waterproof tarpaulins.

Safety Bracing

Safety bracing should be installed before the old roof covering is removed. A simple way to accomplish this is to nail 2 × 4s, horizontally, across the rafters or trusses. Ideally, you should run this bracing across the rafters or trusses at the bottom, center, and near the top. This ties the roof members together to provide strength when the roof sheathing is removed. The bracing should extend from one end of the roof to the other and on both sides of the attic. Without this bracing, the roof members may have little or no support once the roof sheathing is removed.

Removing Shingles

How you remove the shingles depends upon your approach to the job. Many people remove the shingles as one phase of the job. Others remove the shingles and the roof sheathing all at once. If you decide to remove the shingles individually, you'll spend more time on your job.

When removing just the shingles, a common method is scraping. By using a long-handled scraper, you can place the blade of the scraper under the shingles and push them off the roof. You could use a putty knife to lift the edges of the shingles and pull them off, but the heavy-duty scraper will be much faster (when working with asphalt or fibreglass shingles).

If you happen to have a slate or tile roof, the procedure is more difficult. A tin roof is also removed differently. If you want to remove a roof with one of these coverings, consult a local professional for recommended removal procedures. With all phases of your job, keep safety in mind. Wear safety glasses and appropriate clothing and footwear. It's best not to work alone, and always be aware of what is below you as you discard roofing to the ground.

Removing Shingles & Sheathing All at Once

When you remove shingles and sheathing all at once, you save time, and you're able to work from the inside of your attic, instead of from the outside, on the roof. A reciprocating saw is the best tool for this job. A circular saw will work, but it just isn't quite as safe as a reciprocating saw for most users.

Before beginning, block off the area around your home so that no one will be injured by falling debris. Since you'll be inside the attic, you won't be able to see who or what is below. Also, be sure to have the bracing in place on the rafters or trusses.

Once the work area is secure, you'll be ready to remove the roof sheathing and shingles. With a rough, wood-cutting blade in your saw, cut the sheathing, from inside the attic, along the edges of the rafters or trusses. Most rafters and trusses are set on two-foot centers. This means you will be cutting out sections of sheathing that are approximately 2' wide.

It is usually best to cut these 2'-wide pieces out in sections, rather than in their full-length dimension. For example, if your rafters are 18' long, make the length of your cuts about 4'. These smaller pieces are more manageable and create less danger. Remember, even these small pieces are going to be heavy, and they're going to fall somewhere when you cut them loose. If you have a helper, this falling debris shouldn't cause much of a problem, since the second person can hold the debris. If you're working alone, extra caution is required. Once the sheathing and shingles are gone, you're ready to remove the rafters or trusses.

Removing Trusses

Truss removal can be done in several ways. If you're willing to remove the ceilings in the rooms below your attic, the trusses can be lifted off the top of your house in one piece. However, this is usually impractical. It's unlikely that you'll make it through the truss-removal process without damaging the ceilings below, but there is a way to minimize that damage.

The bottom cord of your trusses will be resting on the top of the plate of your house (Illus. 4-4). Add extra nails, normally 16d nails, to make the connection between the bottom cord and the top plate stronger. Once this is done, and your safety bracing is in place, you can cut out sections of the trusses. As you cut out the trusses, leave the bottom cord in place.

The bottom cord will help to maintain the integrity of the ceilings below. The new floor joists that you will be adding will be taller than the bottom cords. Also, the new joists will normally be set on 16″ centers. The bottom cords should be on 24″ centers. This allows you to leave the bottom cords without inhibiting the new joists.

Rafter Removal

Rafter removal is similar to truss removal, but it's generally easier. Rafters and ceiling joists are connected, but they are not an integral unit like trusses. Rafters are normally nailed to a common ridge board. The ridge board is the board that runs the length of your attic, at the peak, and this ridge board allows all of the rafters to lean into it and to be nailed to it.

Rafters are generally notched to rest on the top plate of the house. The rafters are usually nailed both to the top plate and to the ceiling joists (Illus. 4-5). Before removing the rafters, place safety braces under the ridge board. These braces should run from the ceiling joists to the bottom of the ridge board, and they're intended to support the ridge board as the rafters are removed.

Before beginning demolition, add some extra nails to the ceiling joists to hold them to the top plate. Cut blocking for installation between the ceiling joists to minimize twisting and nail pops in the ceilings below.

Start the rafter removal at the point where the rafter connects to the ceiling joist.

Illus. 4-5. Notched rafters

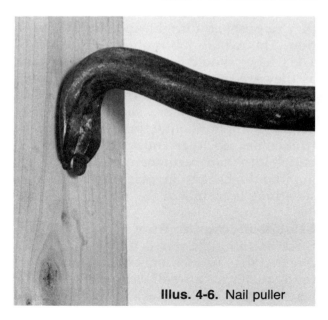

Illus. 4-6. Nail puller

Using a nail-puller (Illus. 4-6), remove the nails holding the rafter to the ceiling joist. Next, remove the nails holding the rafter to the top plate. Then, remove the nails holding the rafter to the horizontal safety bracing. With these nails removed, all that should be left are the nails at the ridge board. Once the ridge-board nails are out, you can lower the rafter to the ground.

Putting on the New Roof

Once you have the old roof removed, you're ready to put on the new one. You have two options. You could either stick-build a new roof or you could install room trusses. Let's examine each procedure.

Room Trusses

If room trusses will serve your needs, they constitute the fastest method to get your new roof on. This procedure will work best if you hire a crane and a crane operator to set the trusses in place for you. If you don't have the benefit of a crane, plan on having some strong bodies to help pull the trusses to the top of the house. The trusses on each end of the house are *gable trusses*. They will be made differently from the rest of the trusses; they're built to allow siding to be installed on them.

Once the trusses are atop the house, they're propped upright and slid into position. This whole job requires extra hands. The trusses should be nailed to the top plate as they are put into place, and they should be braced with 2 × 4s. As the line of trusses gets longer, the trusses should be tied together with horizontal bracing. Once the trusses are up, they must be squared and nailed into their permanent positions. Bracing should be left in place until the roof sheathing is installed.

Stick-Building the Roof

Stick-building the roof is a little more complicated than using room trusses, but it's actually easier for a small work crew (in some ways) than room trusses. Setting the ridge

board is the most strenuous aspect of a stick-built roof.

The first step is to set the ridge board into place. It will have to be held in place with bracing and supports. Once the ridge board is in place, you're ready to install the rafters.

Most professionals figure out the rafter design they want and then cut the rafters while the lumber's still on the ground. The rafter will be notched to rest on the top plate. In the trade, this notch is often called a *bird's-mouth*. The piece of the rafter extending over the side of the house is called the tail, and it forms the overhang. The other end of the rafter will be angled to fit against the ridge board. Once you have cut one rafter that fits properly, you can use it as a template to cut the other rafters.

Once the rafters are cut, set them into place, one at a time. Nail each rafter as you go. The rafter should be nailed to the ridge board, the top plate, and the ceiling joists (Illus. 4-7). You may have to install blocking between the rafter and the ceiling joists.

For the gable ends, you will have to install studs in the area between the rafters. This is simply a matter of cutting 2 × 4s and installing them vertically, on 16" centers. The studs will attach to the top plate and to the bottom of the rafters.

The last step in the roof framing is to install the collar ties. Collar ties are usually made from 2 × 6s or 2 × 8s (Illus. 4-8). These ties are simply short pieces of wood that are nailed between two rafters to tie them together. Each pair of rafters should be connected with a collar tie.

Installing New Sheathing

Now you're ready to install new sheathing. CDX plywood is normally used for roof sheathing, but particleboard is an alternative material. Since roof sheathing isn't normally cut with a tongue-and-groove joint, plywood clips should be used where the sheathing comes together. These H-clips help to maintain the rigidity of the sheath-

Illus. 4-7. Rafter framing

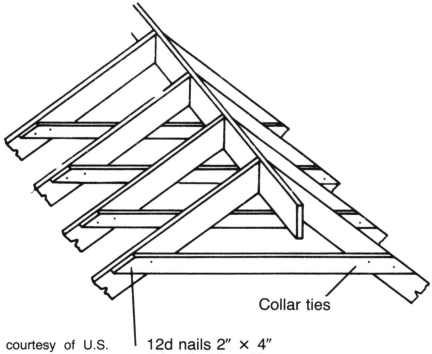

Illus. 4-8. Collar ties. Drawing courtesy of U.S. Dept. of Agriculture

Collar ties

12d nails 2″ × 4″
8d nails 1″ × 6″

ing (Illus. 4-9). The clips should be installed at the midpoint between rafters or trusses.

Installing Roof Covering

Roofing felt is often applied over the roof sheathing, before shingles are applied. Sometimes the felt is omitted and the shingles are applied directly to the sheathing.

The roof flashing and the metal drip-edge are generally installed next, and then the shingles are applied. There is an art to running shingles. With proper planning and the use of chalk lines, you can get an even and attractive roof. A "square" of shingles is the equivalent of 100 square feet. The starter course of shingles will usually extend about

½" over the drip-edge. The edges of the roof will normally have a shingle exposure of about 5".

If you use roofing nails to attach the shingles, use four nails, each 1¼" long, in each strip of shingles. If you use a pneumatic stapler, the staples should have a wide crown and should be 1⅝" long. Make sure your nails or staples penetrate thoroughly and allow the shingles to lie flat. When your roof flashing, drip-edge, and shingles are installed, you will have completed the roofing.

Raising your roof can make quite a difference in the appearance of your home. Not only will raising the roof make a visual difference, it will allow more living space. In some cases you'll have enough room to install a kitchen (Illus. 4-10).

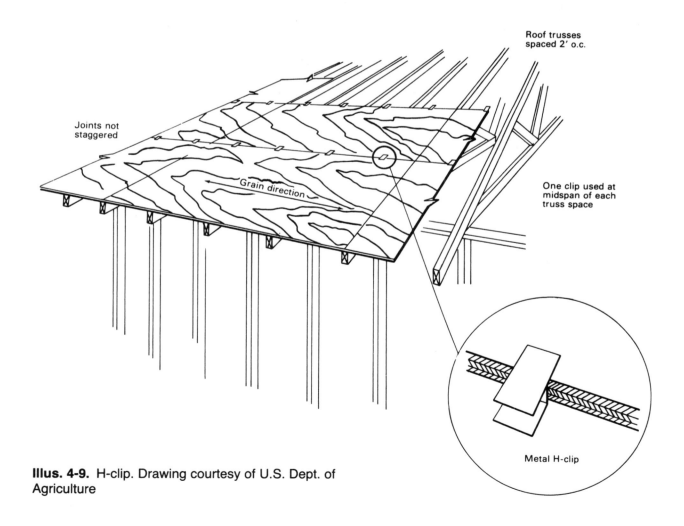

Illus. 4-9. H-clip. Drawing courtesy of U.S. Dept. of Agriculture

Illus. 4-10. Kitchen design. Photo courtesy of Quaker Maid, A Division of WCI, Inc.

5
Reinforcing Second-Floor Joists

With most attic conversions it's necessary to reinforce the second-floor joists. These joists are the floor joists for the attic and the ceiling joists for the rooms below the attic. The joists in most attics are spaced too far apart and they may be too small to be used as floor joists for living space. With these two facts in mind, let's see what can be done about the problems.

Joists That Are Too Small

It's not uncommon to encounter existing attic joists that are too small to support living space, but this shouldn't be a major problem. As an example, assume that your attic has existing joists that are 2 × 6s, 24″ on center. Remember that any excessive disruption in the attic may cause damage to the ceilings below.

In this example, you're planning to add two bedrooms and a bathroom in your attic.

After checking the local building code, you find that to carry this load, you need floor joists that are 2 × 8s, 16″ on center. You currently have 2 × 6 joists, 24″ on center. What will you do? You'll leave the existing joists in place, and add new 2 × 8 joists, 16″ on center.

However, your job may be complicated by existing electrical wires and insulation. Before buying lumber, look for existing obstacles that must be dealt with. If you have electrical wiring running everywhere in your attic floor, you'll have to make adjustments before installing new joists. This could involve just pulling staples and moving loose wiring to a more suitable location, or, you may need an electrician to make the needed adjustments.

If the wiring all runs close to the ceiling of the rooms below, you may be able to use blocking to elevate the new joists above the wiring, if ceiling-height requirements will allow such a rise. To do this, you would install blocking, usually 2 × 4s laid flat on the top plate, to rest the new joists on, creating a shallow chase between the new joists and the ceiling below.

If your attic floor is covered with insulation, remove it; it may be possible to store it for later use.

Some attics have rough flooring nailed to the joists. This flooring must be removed. Again, it may be possible to store and reuse such flooring.

Next, get your new joist material into the workspace. The most difficult part of this procedure may be getting the floor joists into the attic. Since you'll be installing bedrooms in the attic, you'll have to install egress windows. These windows will allow you to get your lumber into the attic without having to go through the finished part of your home. If you already have windows in the gable ends of the attic, you can slide the lumber through those windows. If you don't have windows yet, cut a rough opening for one of the windows and use the opening to pass the lumber through.

You can construct a plywood sliding board to pull the lumber up. You could lay an extension ladder up against the house and use it as a base to hoist the lumber into the attic. If you'll be cutting in a dormer (for the bathroom, for example), you can bring the lumber in through the dormer opening. There are many creative ways to get the new joist material into the attic.

Once the lumber is in the attic, you'll be ready to install the new joists. Cut them to the proper sizes and set them in place. In most cases, you'll use two pieces of wood to span the length of the attic. One end of each joist will rest on the outside plate. The other end of each joist will rest on a bearing partition or beam. When the two joists meet at the bearing point, the lumber should be long enough for each joist to extend past the other. As these two joists lie next to each other, nail them together. The joists should also be nailed to the top plates and to the bearing wall. Once the joists are nailed in place, you should add blocking between the joists, to keep them from twisting.

"Scabbing" Joists Together

Depending upon your structural requirements, you may be able to "scab" new joists onto the existing joists. As always, check with your local code-enforcement office before doing any major work, but this option could save you time and money. If you're allowed to scab new joists onto old joists, you won't have as much work to do. This procedure will require existing joists with dimensions of at least 2″ × 6″.

Your new joists should be the same size as the existing joists. Place the new joists beside the existing joists, and nail the new joists to the top plate, the bearing wall, and the existing joists. When nailing the new joists to the old joists, maintain a regular pattern and interval in your nailing. Nail at the bottom, in the middle, and at the top of each joist, with the horizontal spacing not exceeding 16″. You probably don't need this many nails, but the added nailing will reduce the risk of twisting and weakness.

By doubling the width of your joist with this scabbing procedure, you are increasing the strength of the structural member. When allowed, this is a fast and economical way to reinforce the floor joists.

Joists That Are Too Far Apart

Finding joists that are too far apart to support living space is another common problem. Since most attic joists are spaced 24″ apart, and most floor joists for living spaces are spaced 16″ apart, it's easy to see why this is a problem. If the only problem is that you need the joists closer together, simply add more joists, just as described earlier in this chapter.

Shortening the Span

There are times when the length of the span of the attic joists will create problems. Since much of the roof's weight is supported by the exterior walls, there isn't a heavy de-

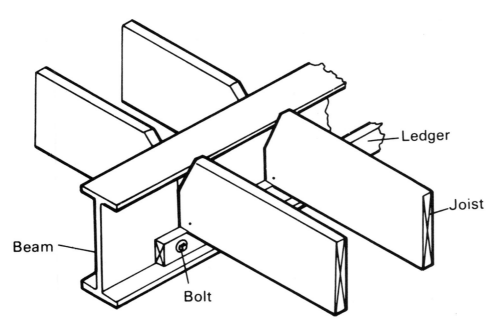

Illus. 5-1. Joists meeting at I-beam. Drawing courtesy of U.S. Dept. of Agriculture

mand on attic joists for weight support. This can cause a significant problem with attic conversions.

The unsupported span of attic joists will depend upon the placement of bearing walls or beams below the joists. It's possible to add bearing walls and beams to increase support and shorten attic spans (Illus. 5-1). However, this will mean some remodelling of the house below the attic.

If you must add support walls or beams, you must have them positioned to rest on a solid foundation. This foundation could be either the house's foundation or pier foundations (Illus. 5-2), installed just for the new bearing support. In any event, the bearing wall or beam must be supported by a solid foundation of adequate strength.

Once the new bearing wall or beam is installed, the attic joists will have a shorter span between unsupported intervals, increasing the strength of the joists.

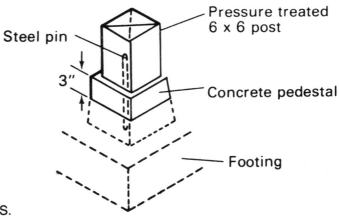

Illus. 5-2. Pier foundation. Drawing courtesy of U.S. Dept. of Agriculture

Minimizing Ceiling Damage

With the use of blocking, you can minimize ceiling damage during an attic conversion. By placing blocking under new floor joists, or between the joists and the top plates, you'll keep the new joists from coming into contact with the existing ceiling. This will prevent ceiling damage, but it doesn't offer any guarantee against nail pops and other types of minor damage.

Adding blocking under new joists means losing ceiling height. Ceiling height is usually low in attic conversions anyway, and blocking could just ruin the ceiling-height requirements. If you want to install your new joists with blocking, you may be able to raise the existing collar ties to pick up some extra height. It may be necessary to use new lumber for the relocated collar ties. Some builders use 2 × 4s for this purpose, but I prefer 2 × 6s. When relocating the collar ties, use three 16d nails in each end, in a triangular pattern.

6
Framing the Walls, Ceilings & Partitions

In any type of conversion project, you'll be likely to deal with framing walls, ceilings, or partitions. Framing isn't particularly difficult, but doing it right isn't as easy as some people think.

What's the difference between a wall and a partition? *Partitions* are interior walls that separate two areas, usually two rooms. *Walls* are most often thought of as a building's exterior framing and load-bearing framing. You'd be correct to call either of these framing structures walls. However, the building trade usually differentiates between exterior walls, load-bearing walls, and interior partitions.

Framing Exterior Walls

Framing exterior walls might be required in either an attic or garage conversion. There are many framing methods, but most professionals build exterior walls and then stand them up and into place. This is the first procedure described here.

Prefab Your Walls

When you build exterior walls, you can usually prefab them. This process allows you to frame the entire wall in comfortable surroundings. The framing is usually done on the subfloor of the structure being built. Here's how it's done.

First, lay out the locations for all the exterior walls by marking the subfloor with a chalk line. Once you have the layout marked, measure the length of the bottom plate. If you're dealing with a long span, you may want to build the wall in sections.

Cut the bottom and top plates to the desired length. If you're building with a standard ceiling height, you can use 2 × 4 studs that are precut to the proper height. If you're working with an unusual ceiling height, cut the wall studs yourself. Remember to allow for the thickness of the top and bottom plates. Most carpenters use one 2 × 4 as a bottom plate and install two 2 × 4s for the top plate.

Once all of the pieces are cut, you'll be ready to prefab the wall. Turn the bottom and top plates over onto their edges. Place your first stud at one end of the plates and nail it into place (Illus. 6-1). Next, do the same with a second stud, at the other end. Many pros use air-powered nailing guns (Illus. 6-2 and Illus. 6-3), but a regular hammer will do the job. Once the two ends are nailed, check to make sure that the framework is square. Then, install the remainder of the studs. Wall studs are typically installed with 16″ between them, from center to center. Use two nails in each end of the studs.

When the wall section is complete, you'll be ready to put it into place. If you're working with a large wall section, you'll need some help standing it up and getting it in place. Some carpenters just stand the walls up and nail them into place. Others take time to place wood blocks on the band board as a safety feature. By taking 2 × 4s, about 18″ long, and nailing them to the band board

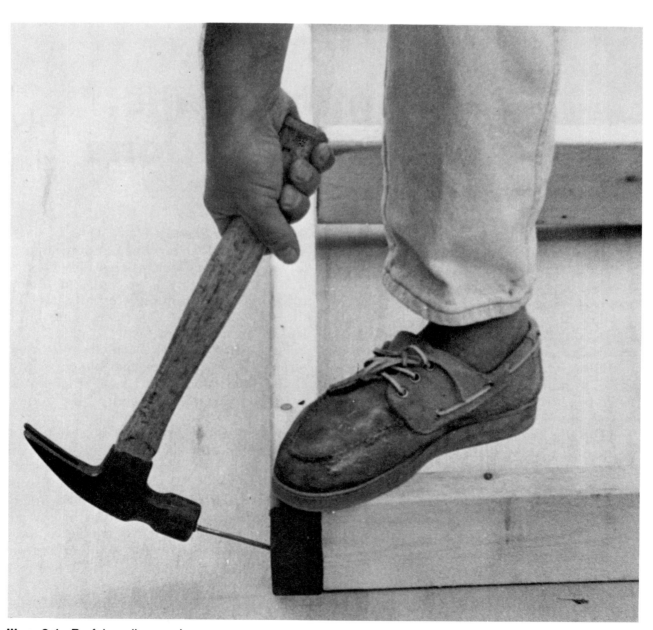

Illus. 6-1. Prefab wall procedure

Illus. 6-2. Air-powered nailing gun

so that they stick up past the subfloor, you'll have a bumper to butt the wall section into. This bumper makes it easier for a small crew to stand up large walls and it reduces the risk of the wall section falling off the framing platform.

Another step to take before standing up your wall is to install prop braces. These prop braces are just long 2 × 4s nailed to the ends of the wall section. These braces will hold the wall up, once it's standing. You'll also need some blocks of wood to nail in behind the braces, where they rest on the subfloor. With large wall sections, you should prepare braces in the middle of the wall, and possibly at intervals between the middle and end braces.

Once the wall is standing, position the braces to support the wall. The end of the brace should be resting on the subfloor. Nail

Illus. 6-3. Nails for an air-powered nailing gun

a block of wood to the subfloor to prevent the brace from moving. Next, nail the bottom plate to the subfloor and floor joists.

Prefab Knee Walls

When you want to prefab knee walls, the procedure is a little different. Knee walls are meant to rest on a flat subfloor and to tie into the rafters above. This means that the top plate for a knee wall won't be flat, as it would with a normal exterior wall. The top plate must be angled to fit the pitch of the roof rafters. There are two common kinds of prefab construction for this type of wall.

You can cut the wall studs on an angle that will allow the top plate to be in alignment with the rafters. The prefab procedure is about the same as that described earlier. Cut the top and bottom plates. Figure the angle needed for the wall studs and cut those studs. Then, nail the section together. From there, you simply stand the wall up and nail it to the rafters, subfloor, and floor joists. Remember to check the wall alignment before nailing the knee wall into place permanently.

The other way of building a prefab knee-wall doesn't use a traditional top plate. First, cut the bottom plate and tack it into position. Then, using a plumb bob or a stud and a level, mark the bottom plate for proper stud placement. Keep in mind that for this type of framing your studs will be nailed into the sides of the rafters. Therefore, when marking the bottom plate, you must have the stud located so it will stand next to a rafter.

When you've marked all of the stud locations on the bottom plate, remove the plate from the subfloor. Cut the studs so that they'll be long enough to reach from the bottom plate to a point above the rafter, allowing the stud to be nailed to the rafter.

Nail the studs to the plate, just as you would in any prefab situation. Next, stand the wall up and get it in the desired position. Check alignment and nail the bottom plate in place. Then, nail the studs to the rafters, but check each stud with a level as you go. It is easy for this type of wall to get out of square.

When the wall is secure, cut 2 × 4 blocking to install between the studs. This blocking will be nailed horizontally between the studs, providing a nailing surface similar to a top plate. If you don't like cutting angles, this method will work best, but the angled method is the choice of most pros.

Toenail Methods

You could use toenail methods to frame your wall, but these methods are generally more difficult and not very strong. In the case of a knee wall, you could cut each stud on an angle to mate with the rafters. Then, you could nail the stud to the face of the rafter, rather than to the side. On regular walls, you could erect the top and bottom plates and toenail the studs between them, but I can't imagine why you would want to.

Partitions

Partitions will be framed using the same basic procedures already described for walls. Partitions are typically held in place with nails driven into floor joists, ceiling joists, and connection points with adjoining walls. These connection points are frequently those places where studs have been doubled up, to allow a better nailing surface for the connection. Some carpenters use wood blocking between the studs of exterior walls to allow a nailing surface for partition walls.

Basement Walls

The exterior walls of basements are usually made of concrete or masonry material. The floors in basements and garages are normally concrete. The walls in basements are often uneven. These walls offer little opportunity for insulation. In daylight basements there are generally ledges that run around the entire basement, about 4' above the floor. This ledge is the result of the thick concrete wall giving way to the thinner wood-framed wall of the daylight section. All of these peculiarities call for different framing techniques.

Attaching Walls to Concrete Floors

There are three basic ways to attach wood walls to concrete floors. First, you could use a drill bit to drill into the concrete. Once the hole is drilled, you could insert a plastic anchor that would accept a screw, allowing you to screw the wall plate to the concrete floor. As the screw goes into the anchor, the anchor expands to hold the screw firmly. This method works, but it's very time-consuming.

The second method uses concrete nails to attach the walls to the concrete floor. Safety glasses are a must for this procedure. Nails meant for use with concrete are brittle and they frequently shatter.

The third method uses a powder-activated device to drive special nails through the wood and into the concrete. The large construction-grade tools can be rented; small inexpensive versions can be purchased. In the small version, insert one of the special nails into the barrel of the device (Illus. 6-4). Then, put a small rimfire powder cartridge into the chamber of the tool (Illus. 6-5 and Illus. 6-6). Wear gloves, ear protection, and eye protection (Illus. 6-7) when using this tool. Next, place the end of the barrel (of the tool) where you want the nail to be driven. Then, hit the top of the tool with a heavy hammer (Illus. 6-8) and BOOM, your nail is driven.

These tools are great, but they can be dangerous. Read and abide by all of the manufacturer's suggestions when operating these tools and when you buy nails and powder cartridges.

When you attach wood to concrete floors, use pressure-treated lumber. The concrete will give off moisture that can be absorbed by untreated wood. Over time, this moisture may rot untreated wood.

Furring Basement Walls

If you aren't concerned about adding heavy insulation to your existing basement walls, use furring strips to prepare the walls for wall coverings. Coat the masonry or concrete walls with a moisture sealant before installing new walls over the existing ones.

Furring strips should be attached to the concrete wall using adhesive and nails. The same tool used to shoot nails into the floor will also work on the walls.

If the basement walls are uneven, place shims behind the furring strips. Use a level to determine when the furring strips are in the proper position, and then secure the strips to the wall.

When you want to add insulation, but you don't need much, use foam boards to insulate between the furring strips. This insulation can be attached to the concrete basement walls using an adhesive.

Building False Walls

When existing basement walls are *very* uneven, or if you need to add heavy insulation, building false walls is your best approach

See color plate E for a view of such a wall. This is done by framing walls, as mentioned earlier in the chapter, and nailing them to the floor and to the ceiling joists. This will give you a wall with full depth for insulation, plumbing, wiring, and heat. It also allows you to have a straight and even wall surface.

Working with Ledges

In daylight basements it's common for a ledge to run around the perimeter of the basement. This type of wall can be dealt with in two ways.

You could frame a new wall between the ledge and the ceiling joists to give you a

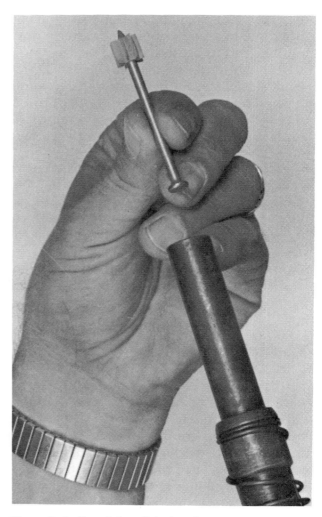

Illus. 6-4. Special nail being inserted in powder-actuated nailer

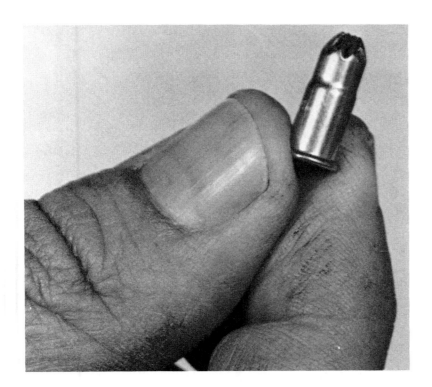

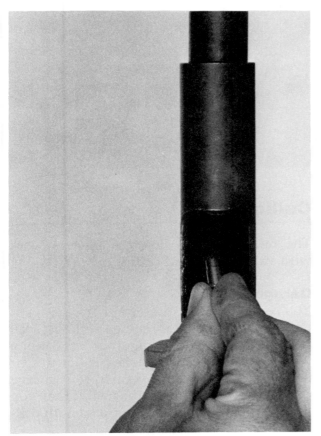

Illus. 6-5. Rimfire cartridge for a powder-actuated nailer

Illus. 6-6. Rimfire cartridge for a powder-actuated nailer being inserted

Illus. 6-7. Safety glasses. Model: Fran Pagurko

Illus. 6-8. Using a powder-actuated nailer

straight, vertical wall. But, if you do this, any existing windows will be set deep into the wall, requiring window boxes. Some people like this look, and they enjoy having the window box to display decorative items.

If you don't want the window box, you can leave the ledge and trim it out with an attractive trim board. This gives you a finished ledge that can serve to hold everything from collectibles to cocktails.

Your basement can serve many needs. It could be an exercise room, an office, a game room, a family room, a den, or whatever your heart desires. The color sections (plates A, F, G, H, I) show some of these basement conversions.

Ceilings

The following will describe how to work with various types of ceiling.

Garage Ceilings
You're likely to encounter either of two situations when framing garage ceilings. You may not have any framing to do at all when you already have ceiling joists, collar ties, or truss bands in place. Look up in your garage to see if there's framing that will allow you to attach to a flat surface, for a smooth ceiling.

If you're converting the lower level of the garage, you shouldn't have to do any addi-

Illus. 6-9. Acoustical tile ceiling. Photo by the makers of Armstrong ceiling materials

Illus. 6-10. Imitation plank ceiling. Photo by the makers of Armstrong ceiling materials

Illus. 6-11. Nailing metal framework in place. Photo by the makers of Armstrong ceiling materials

tional framing for the ceiling. If you're converting the attic of the garage, you may already have collar ties that will allow you to install a finished ceiling. If you don't have a flat surface framed up, you can simply nail collar ties across the rafters to make a flat ceiling. This procedure allows easy installation of a finished ceiling. You might use dry-

wall, acoustic tile (Illus. 6-9), or tongue-and-groove imitation planks (Illus. 6-10).

If you choose ceiling tiles or planks, installation can be easy and quick. Simply nail a metal framework to the joists (Illus. 6-11), and hang the ceiling material (Illus. 6-12 and Illus. 6-13). Small metal tabs hold the ceiling material in place (Illus. 6-14).

Attic Ceilings

Attic ceilings are similar to the ceilings in the upper level of garages. If you don't already have suitable framing for a ceiling, add collar ties to solve your problem. Even if you choose to hang your ceiling directly to the rafters to create a vaulted ceiling, remember the need for proper ventilation. Install collar ties high on the rafters in a vaulted ceiling to allow a small flat ceiling for ventilation.

Basement Ceilings

Basements have ceilings that may be littered with pipes, wiring, and ducts, resulting in low head clearance. Here's how to work around some of the problems common to basement ceilings.

Pipes

Pipes sometimes run beneath the ceiling joists in unfinished basements. Many home-owners see these pipes and automatically as-

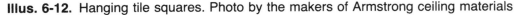

Illus. 6-12. Hanging tile squares. Photo by the makers of Armstrong ceiling materials

Illus. 6-13. Hanging a plank ceiling. Photo by the makers of Armstrong ceiling materials

sume that they must install a hanging ceiling to hide the pipes, but this isn't always necessary.

If you're willing to go to the trouble and expense, most pipes can be relocated and raised to be hidden among the joists. Some drain pipes are so large that raising them would be impossible, but most pipes *can* be raised. If it isn't too expensive, it will be worthwhile to make the necessary adjustments to allow for the installation of a standard ceiling. Real estate appraisers are not kind to cheap, amateur-looking hanging ceilings. However, some very impressive ceiling options that are available if the pipes can *not* be moved are discussed in chapter 14.

Wires

Wires are frequently stapled to the bottom of the ceiling joists in basements. These wires could be moved up and along the joists, but there's an easier way to hide them by dropping down the ceiling joists, using furring strips. The furring strips will allow a chase for the wires, while allowing the installation of a traditional ceiling.

Ducts

Ducts that hang from basement ceiling joists aren't very easy to hide. There *are* ways to improve the looks of these metal monsters. If you have ducts, there will be one large trunk line that runs most of the length of your basement. This large duct must stay below the joists and it must be boxed in.

The smaller supply-and-return ducts can usually fit in the space between joists. It may take a little cutting and metal bending, but you can move most of these small ducts. Be careful of the ducts' sharp edges.

The holes remaining in the trunk line (from the relocated ducts) can be covered with new sheet metal that's held in place with screws. Before you attempt such a renovation of your heating system, consult a heating or plumbing expert to be sure that you won't harm the heating system.

Beams

Beams in the basement are unwanted, but usually needed. One way to make the most of a beam is to box it in and install recessed lighting in the box.

You can build a false box around the beam and attach the box to the ceiling joists, allowing you to make the box any reasonable size that you like. If you prefer to simply wrap the beam, drill holes in it with a high-quality drill bit. Wear eye protection and be aware that the metal shavings will be hot. Bolt 2 × 4s to the beam and create a box just slightly larger than it. Then attach drywall to the wood and cover the beam with a close-fitting box.

Illus. 6-14. Metal tabs used to hold a ceiling in place. Photo by the makers of Armstrong ceiling materials

7
Windows, Skylights & Doors

Windows, skylights, and doors can make the difference between a mediocre conversion and an outstanding one. Natural light and good ventilation are both critical to a pleasant environment. With the proper selection and use of windows, skylights, and doors, your home can be a showplace!

Windows

Windows are no longer just simple pieces of glass held in place by small pieces of wood. Today's windows offer features that can save you money on fuel, and they're designed to make cleaning easy. You can have windows that push up, roll out, or tilt in. There are even windows that don't require painting!

Casement Windows
Casement windows are known for their energy-efficient qualities. These windows are easy to clean from the inside, and they

offer full airflow. When you crank out a casement window, the entire window opens.

These practical and attractive windows can be used almost anywhere. You can build a picture window with them. You can frame a bay window with them and insert a window seat to enjoy the view and the open air. Decorative transoms can be installed above casement windows to add a touch of elegance.

Double-Hung Windows
These windows have endured the test of time. Today, double-hung windows have many new qualities, including tilting sashes and removable grids for easy cleaning, along with high-efficiency ratings for minimum heat loss; vinyl cladding means low maintenance.

Octagonal Windows
Octagonal windows are ideal for bathrooms and stairways. These appealing windows are available either openable or fixed. The glass

selections allow for numerous designs and colors. These handy windows shed light on the smallest of areas.

Awning Windows

These windows open out and up, allowing air circulation, even during gentle rains. When closed, these windows (if grouped together) form a wall of glass. Due to their nature, awning windows can be placed above eye level, to allow for fresh air and privacy at the same time.

Bay & Bow Windows

Bay and bow windows are available in prefab units. They're simple to install, and they're available with a combination of stationary and movable glass.

Skylights

Skylights are ideal for letting light into your attic conversion. Whether you want a model that opens or one that's fixed, there are many to choose from.

What's the difference between a skylight and a roof window? Skylights are mounted in the roof, normally beyond arm's reach. Roof windows on the other hand, are installed in the side of a roof, to allow views of the grounds and of distant scenery. Roof windows are within easy reach and offer many advantages over regular windows and dormers.

Roof Windows

Roof windows are an excellent choice for attic conversions. These special windows let in a lot of light, yet they can be equipped in various ways to control the amount of light. These windows are available in a multitude of sizes, for any need. They are easier to install than gable dormers, and they allow for broader views and more light than gable dormers do.

These versatile windows can be purchased to swing out or tilt in. Some models rotate to facilitate cleaning. Used in a bathroom, the large open area vents the bathroom and removes moisture quickly. There are models available that are sized to meet the requirements for emergency egress when used in a bedroom. Most roof windows are available with screens, so you can enjoy the open air without bugs. The color insert (plates K, L, M, N, O, P, S, AA, FF) shows several versions of skylight and roof window.

Skylights

Skylights have matured since the days of the Plexiglas bubble (Illus. 7-1). These bubbles are still available, and they're a very affordable way to brighten an attic.

Illus. 7-1. Bubble skylight. Photo courtesy of Skymaster skylights, venting or nonventing

Illus. 7-2. New entry door on a Colonial-style house

Modern skylights open, have built-in shades available, and can be equipped with screens. They are also available with insulation features not found in older skylights. There are even control options available that will close the skylight for you if it starts to rain. Some windows can be controlled with a keypad. There are even special rods, some even motorized, that allow you to operate out-of-reach skylights. Color plate R shows such a rod.

Exterior Doors

The options for exterior doors are staggering. You can choose from wood, metal, glass, and fibreglass; the numerous styles and designs could fill a book.

Standard Entry Doors

Standard entry doors are normally 3' wide and hinge on one side. The choices available in entry doors are numerous. Illus. 7-2 shows a new entry door.

Metal Insulated Doors

Metal insulated doors are a good choice for most applications; they're available as solid doors, solid doors stamped to give the appearance of six-panel doors, and with half of the door made of glass, with or without grids. All of these doors are very affordable and perform well.

Wood Doors

Wood doors provide beauty that can't be found in other types of door. The carvings and designs on these doors range from modest to ornate. Wooden doors generally cost more than metal insulated doors, but they can be stained as metal doors cannot.

Wood does have its drawbacks. The insulating quality of a wood door won't match that of an insulated door. Wood doors will also swell in damp weather. This swelling can cause the door to stick or to latch improperly.

Fibreglass Doors

Fibreglass doors are available in many designs; some can even be stained. These doors provide a good "wood" appearance, without the swelling and with better insulating qualities than wood.

Glass Doors

Glass doors are available in various types of frame materials. These doors allow light to flood the interior, but they lack insulating and security properties.

Doors for the Deck or the Patio

If you will be adding a patio, balcony or deck to your newly converted space (Illus. 7-3), the doors will play an important role.

French Doors

French doors are almost completely glass, divided by grilles. Both panels of a double French door open. These doors can be very expensive.

Gliders & Sliders

Sliding glass doors have long been known as "sliders" and "patio doors." Sliders are still available, and they are an appropriate choice in some circumstances. As with most products, the quality of these doors determines how well they work.

Better-quality doors are gliders, which are constructed of high-quality materials and with different techniques from those used in the common slider. Gliders also offer more aesthetic options.

Hinged Patio Doors

Known by many names, the hinged patio door is a double-door unit where only one panel opens. The second panel is fixed and remains sealed at all times. These doors have gained popularity because of their energy efficiency and ease of operation.

False wall in a basement. Photo courtesy of Georgia-Pacific Corp.

E

Basement office. Photo courtesy of Georgia-Pacific
Corp.   F

Basement exercise room. Photo courtesy of
Georgia-Pacific Corp.

G

Basement family room. Photo courtesy of Georgia-Pacific Corp.

H

Illus. 7-3. The advantages of a deck off an attic conversion. Photo courtesy of Lis King and Environmental Graphics

Technical Considerations

When you shop for windows, skylights, and doors, here are some technical points you must consider.

Tempered Glass

If the unit you're buying will be installed in a location where there's a risk that it may be broken, tempered glass should be used.

R-Value

The R-value is a rating assigned to identify the amount of resistance a material has to heat flow. The higher the R-value, the better the insulating value.

U-Value

U-value, not as well known as R-value, is a rating assigned to determine the total heat flow through a unit. A unit with a low U-value has better insulating qualities than does a unit with a higher U-value.

UV Blockage

The UV-blockage rating of a unit indicates how much ultraviolet rays are reduced when they pass through the unit. The higher the UV-blockage rating, the better.

Other Considerations

Most other considerations are matters of taste and money. By looking at cutaway sections such as the one shown in color plate Q, and at product information, it will be fairly easy to compare products. Each brand will boast its own special features. It's your decision which features you'd be willing to pay for.

Installation

Installation depends largely on the type of unit you purchase. For specific installation instructions, refer to and follow the manufacturer's suggested methods. The basic steps for installation are described below.

Framing for Windows

Framing for windows is not difficult, once you know the size to make the rough opening. When you decide which style, type, and brand of window you'll be using, you can get the rough-opening dimension from your supplier. The rough-opening dimension will be larger than the actual window.

When framing for a window, you'll frame an opening in the wall with the use of jack studs, cripple studs, and a header (Illus. 7-4). The header may be made from lumber nailed together, or nailed with spacers between the boards, to make up the proper width. The jack studs will be installed under the header, to hold it up. The jack studs are nailed to standard wall studs, and the header rests on the tops of the jack studs. The header is nailed to the wall studs.

A horizontal board is installed below the header, at a distance equal to the rough-opening dimension. This board is nailed to the wall studs and is supported with and nailed to short studs, from below. The area above the header is filled with cripple studs. These cripple studs extend from the header to the top plate, completing the window frame.

Framing for Exterior Doors

Framing for exterior doors is similar to the process for framing windows. Most doors are available as prehung units; they come to the site ready to be set into the framed opening. When the door comes prehung, framing is done using the same procedure as is used to frame a window, with one exception. The rough door opening should extend all the way to the subfloor. The header, jack studs, and upper cripples will be installed the same as they would be on a window. But, the lower framing done with a window is eliminated, and the section of the bottom wall plate that runs through the door opening is cut out.

Illus. 7-4. Rough window frame

Framing for Skylights

Framing for skylights is usually very easy. Most skylights are made to fit between a pair of rafters. In some cases, all you have to do is nail two boards between the rafters to form a box for the skylight. If the skylight is extra large, you may have to "head off" a rafter and frame out a box.

If you "head off" a rafter, the first step is to cut the rafter. Once the rafter has a section cut out of it, nail a board between the two closest rafters, not counting the one you just cut. This board should be of the same dimension as the rafters and it should butt flush with the rafter you cut. Nail the board to the two intact rafters, first. Then, place a joist hanger under the cut rafter and nail the joist hanger to the header board. Repeat this process for the other cut end of the rafter.

When it's complete, you'll have a large opening. The next step is to frame this large opening into a size that's right for your skylight. This is often done by framing a box between the rafters and headers. Color plate Q shows the framing for a skylight, and an installed skylight.

Installing Windows

The methods used for installing windows will vary, but most windows are easy to install. If your rough opening is plumb and the right size, your windows should be easy to install. Assuming the windows have a nailing flange, and most do, set the window in the rough opening and make sure the window is plumb. Then, nail the window in place by driving nails through the flange. The flange should be on the *exterior* of the house.

Installing Doors

The procedure for installing doors is more difficult than that for installing windows, but it isn't that bad. Set the prehung door unit in place. Level it (Illus. 7-5), and place shims between the framed opening and the jamb (Illus. 7-6 and Illus. 7-7) as needed. When the door is plumb, nail the jamb to the framed opening (Illus. 7-8).

Skylight Installation

Skylight installation is normally a matter of placing the skylight in the opening, from the outside, and nailing the flange to the framing members. Some types of skylight will have moulded nailing flanges that are designed to be set down over the edge of a 2 × 4. With this type of flange, the framing must include a raised rim for the skylight to sit on. Once the skylight is placed on the raised box, nails will be driven through the flange and into the box material.

Flashing

Flashing is what keeps water from leaking past the installed unit. Many units come with flashing material already in place, but some don't. Be sure that the proper flashing is installed with your unit.

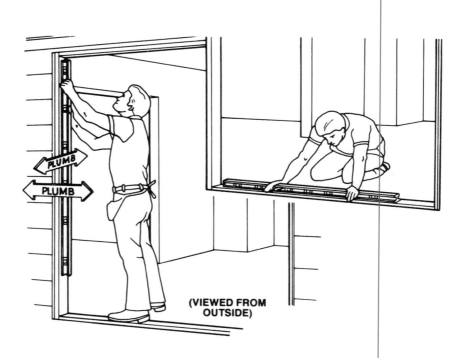

(VIEWED FROM OUTSIDE)

Illus. 7-5. Levelling a door. Drawing courtesy of Morgan Products, Ltd.

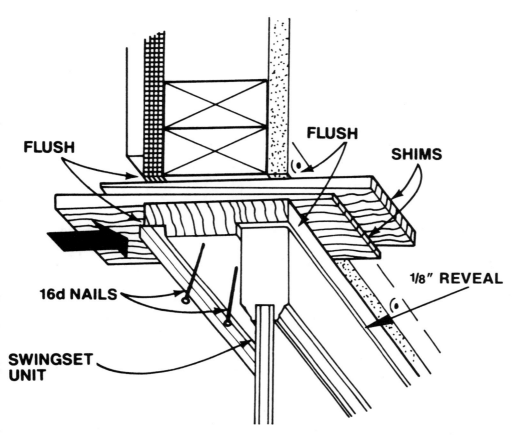

FLUSH

FLUSH

SHIMS

16d NAILS

1/8" REVEAL

SWINGSET
UNIT

SECTION THRU HEAD SHOWING SHIMS

Illus. 7-6. Installing shims. Drawing courtesy of
Morgan Products, Ltd.

SHIMS

**PLUMB
AND NAIL
FIXED
HEIGHT
SIDE
FIRST**

DOOR

Illus. 7-7. Installing shims. Drawing courtesy of Morgan Products, Ltd.

Illus. 7-8. Nailing the doorjamb. Drawing courtesy of Morgan Products, Ltd.

8
Stairways

When choosing a stairway for your conversion project, consider all of the options. Some stairs are more attractive than others; some stairs are more practical. Stair design can hinder furniture movement. Code requirements must be considered when choosing a stairway. This chapter will show you the most commonly used stairs and some exotic options. In addition, you'll learn about code considerations, framing methods, and railing designs.

Designs for railings are even more diversified than those for the stairs themselves. The materials you choose for your railing and associated trim can add thousands of dollars to the cost of your project.

Choosing a Stair Design

Choosing a stair design is an aspect of your job that deserves careful attention. Whether descending to a basement family room or ascending to an attic getaway, the stairs will be in constant use. The wrong design can be frustrating, fatiguing, or even dangerous. Some options follow below.

Straight Stairs

Straight stairs are just that. These are the most common and the most economical stairs. However, this design can be steep and fatiguing, as well as boring.

Stairs with Winders

Stairs with winders are not uncommon (Illus. 8-1). This stair design can be installed in an area that's shorter than the area needed for a set of straight stairs. The winders provide a place to take a break, relieving fatigue. Stairs with winders can be a simple design, using only a winder at the base of the stairs, or they can be intricate, with many winders and changes in direction.

Spiral Stairs

Spiral stairs are interesting and distinctive. These stairs can be installed in a minimum of space, but many people have trouble navigating spiral stairs. Furniture movement is another problem with spiral stairs. These stairs are fine as a second means of access, but they should be avoided as the sole access whenever possible.

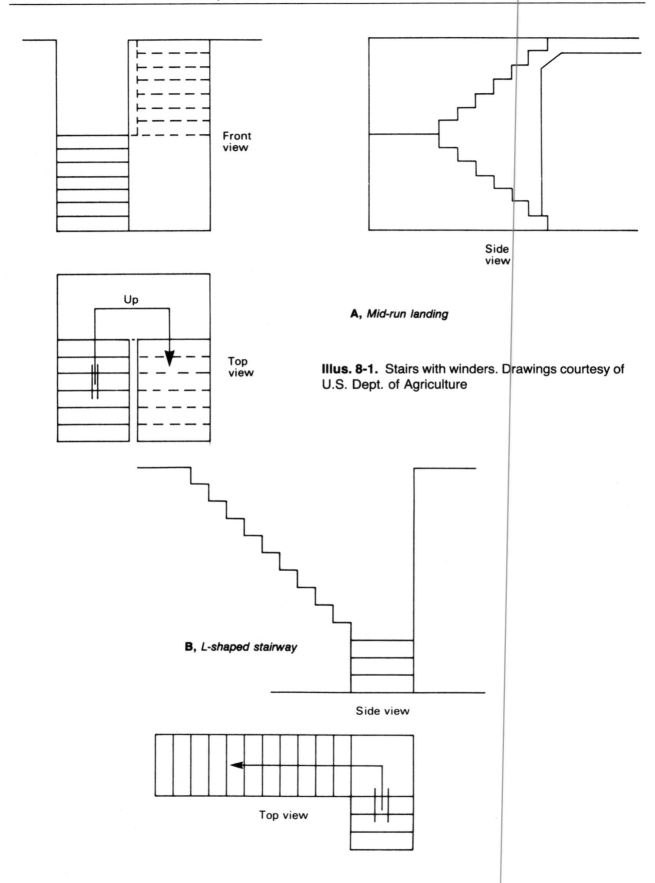

Front view

Side view

Up

Top view

A, *Mid-run landing*

Illus. 8-1. Stairs with winders. Drawings courtesy of U.S. Dept. of Agriculture

B, *L-shaped stairway*

Side view

Top view

Sweeping Stairs

Sweeping stairs seem to roll downwards regally. These curving stairs flow like a gentle river, meandering to their destination. This design is impressive but expensive. Not only is the stair construction expensive, but the wall construction needed to follow the curving design adds extra costs.

Open-Tread Stairs

Open-tread stairs are good for maintaining an open, spacious feeling in a room, but such stairs can be dangerous. The open design doesn't have a toe-kick, so people occasionally miss their footing and fall.

Railings

There are numerous railing options. You could choose a conservative railing, or you could spend thousands of dollars on an artistic railing ensemble. The first consideration when choosing railings depends upon your choice of stairway construction. If, for example, the stairs will be enclosed on both sides by walls, you can choose an inexpensive handrail. When the stairs are open on both sides, you must install railings on both sides. Some railing options are listed below.

Basic Handrail

The basic handrail is a straight piece of finished wood that's attached to the wall by brackets. The handrail may be round, square, or shaped into a design.

Illus. 8-2. Here's an example of a half-wall rail

Handrails Used with Balusters

Handrails used with balusters tend to be much more expensive, much larger and much more ornate than basic handrails. Component parts are used in conjunction with these handrails to create an attractive assembly. The component parts and balusters can be costly, but there are numerous options, so you can design the look you want.

Half-Wall Rails

Half-wall rails are often used on the open side of stairs. When one side of the stairs is protected by a full wall, a half wall is often built on the unprotected side. This wall is built at the height required by local codes for a handrail, and is capped with a finished trim board. This type of stair protection is cost-effective and offers good protection for small children. Illus. 8-2 shows such a rail.

Code Considerations

Since local codes vary, check with your local code-enforcement authorities before building your stairs. The important questions to ask are these:

What's the maximum riser height (Illus. 8-3)?

What's the minimum stair width?

What's the minimum tread depth (Illus. 8-4)?

What's the minimum width between handrails?

What's the minimum clearance requirement for headroom?

How high should the handrail be?

How many handrails are required?

How much space is allowed between balusters?

How deep should platforms be?

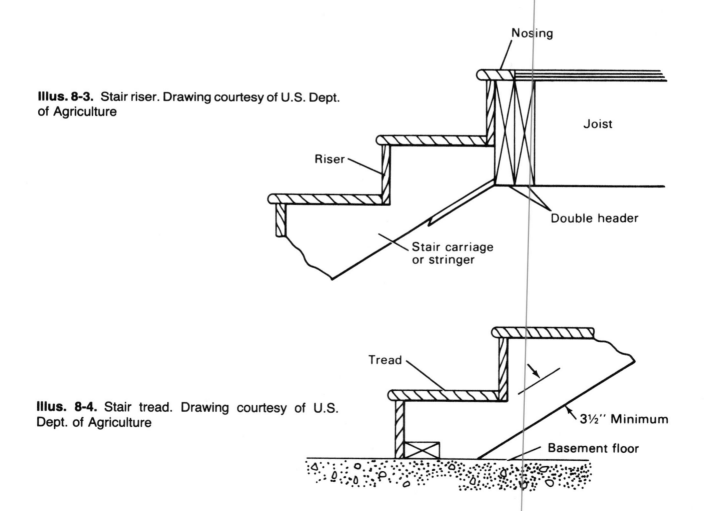

Illus. 8-3. Stair riser. Drawing courtesy of U.S. Dept. of Agriculture

Illus. 8-4. Stair tread. Drawing courtesy of U.S. Dept. of Agriculture

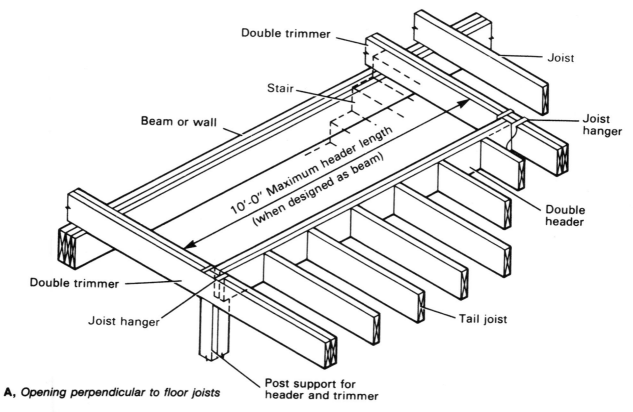

A, *Opening perpendicular to floor joists*

Illus. 8-5. Perpendicular stair opening. Drawing courtesy of U.S. Dept. of Agriculture

Illus. 8-6. Parallel stair opening. Drawing courtesy of U.S. Dept. of Agriculture

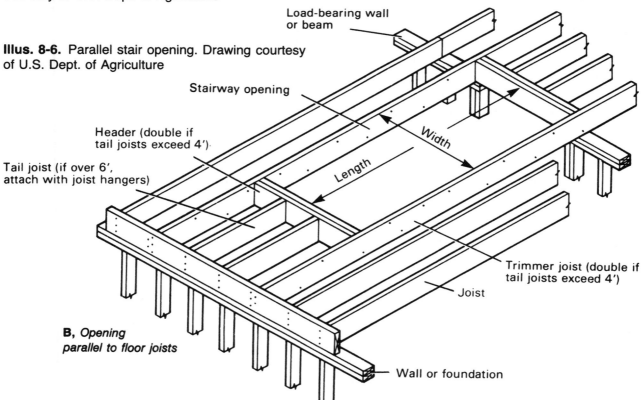

B, *Opening parallel to floor joists*

Framing the Stairs

The framing for the stairs will depend on local codes and the type of stairs you're building or installing. Spiral stairs come ready to set into your framed opening. Finished wood stairs are available in prefab sets. You might be framing rough steps that will be covered with carpet. If you're installing prefab stairs, frame according to the manufacturer's suggestions. If you're building your own steps, follow the guidelines of your local building code.

Framing Straight Stairs

Framing straight stairs requires thought, but it's a task that those with some carpentry skills can accomplish. The first step is to pick the location of the stairs. Ideally, you should choose a place where the stairs will run *with* the floor joists. If the stairs will be installed to run *perpendicular* to the floor joists (Illus. 8-5 and Illus. 8-6), there will be much extra work involved.

Once you've chosen the location, make the rough opening for your stairs. This will involve cutting existing floor joists. The floor joists you cut must be headed off. If you are forced to cut many joists, it may be necessary to add some type of temporary support below the joists. It may also be necessary to install a permanent support below the altered joists.

When you have your rough opening framed in, you'll be ready to lay out the stairs. Measure the vertical distance between the two floors where the stairs will be going. Your measurements should allow for the thickness of the finished floor covering. When you have this measurement, divide it by the height you plan to make each riser. For example, if you are going to have 7″ risers, divide your vertical measurement by seven. This will tell you how many steps you'll have.

When you design the stairs, it's important to use a good ratio between riser height and tread width. When you combine the height of a riser with the width of a tread, the total of the two numbers should be around 17½″. A typical design might be 7″ risers and 10½″ treads. The combination can work in many variations, as long as you stay within code requirements. You could have a 7½″ riser and a 10″ tread.

When building the stairs, a 2 × 4 spacer is usually installed on the stud wall for the stair stringer to attach to. This makes hanging drywall easier and reduces airflow that might be a factor in a fire. The 2 × 4 is nailed to the wall studs at the same angle used by the stringer. Another 2 × 4 should be installed in front of the stringers. This 2 × 4 is called a cleat, and it provides a place for the stringers to attach to the subfloor.

Stair stringers (or "carriages") are normally made with 2 × 12s (Illus. 8-7). A framing square is used to draw the lines for cutting out the riser spaces. Put the framing square on the stringer board with the short arm of the square hitting the top of the board at the desired riser height. Angle the square until the long arm reaches a point equal to the tread dimension. Mark these locations by tracing along the square. Continue this process, with the square intersecting each previous mark, until all riser cuts are marked.

Trim the thickness of a single tread from the bottom of the stringer. Notch the bottom of the stringer to sit on the cleat or kicker plate (Illus. 8-8). The top of the stringer must be notched to rest on a ledger or in a joist hanger. You can nail a ledger to the stairway header for the stringers to rest on, or you can use metal joist hangers to support the stringers.

Once you've cut the first stringer, test it to see if the measurements are correct. If they are, use the stringer you've already cut as a template to cut the other stringers. Most stairways should have three stringers, one on each end and one in the middle. After the stringers are installed, you'll be ready to put the risers and treads in place. Install the risers first and the treads last.

Illus. 8-7. Stair framing detail. Drawing courtesy of U.S. Dept. of Agriculture

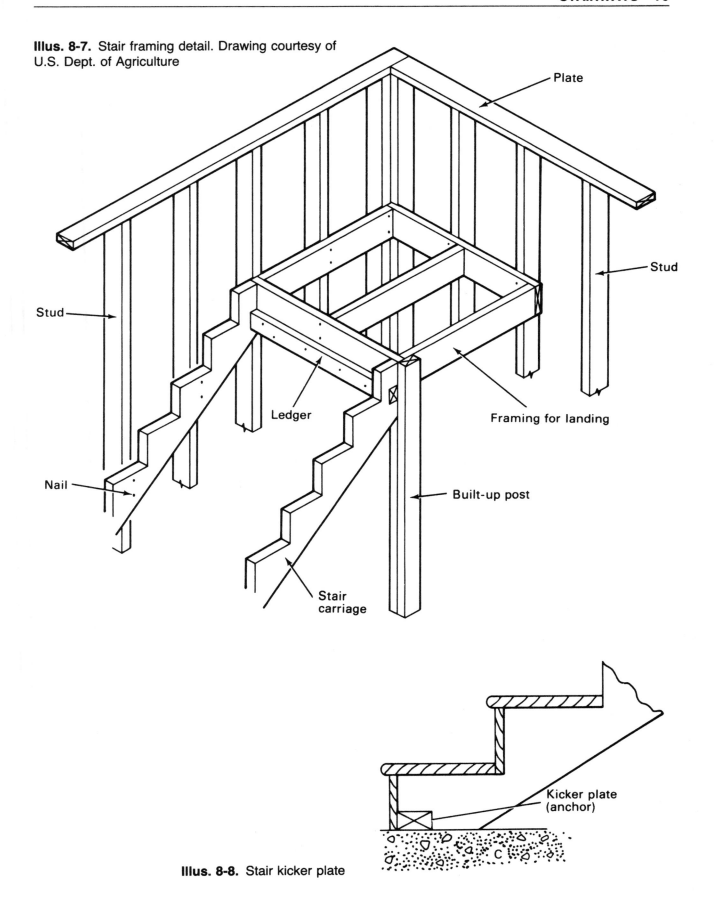

Plate

Stud

Stud

Ledger

Framing for landing

Nail

Built-up post

Stair carriage

Illus. 8-8. Stair kicker plate

Kicker plate (anchor)

Adding Winders

If you'll be adding winders to the stairs, treat each winder platform as a different floor level. Compute the stair height from the platform to the finished floor. If the stair design gets too complicated, don't hesitate to call in a professional.

Outside Stairs

When garage attics are converted to living space, the stairs for the new space are sometimes installed along the outside wall of the garage. This saves space in the building, but it can hurt the appraised value of your improvement. It's better to build the stairs *inside* the garage.

9
Adding a Dormer

Adding a dormer is a good way both to expand an attic and to let more light into the space. Dormers can be used to create space for bedrooms, bathrooms, or just for windows. Adding a dormer is a rather large undertaking, but it is a manageable project for homeowners with some mechanical talent.

There are two basic types of dormer. A gable dormer (Illus. 9-1) is used primarily to provide space for a window. This type of dormer is particularly popular on Cape Cod–style homes. Roof windows may be a better alternative for this purpose, if your only goal is to get good light and ventilation in your attic. Color plate C shows a house with roof windows. However, many people prefer the appearance of gable dormers.

The other basic type of dormer is a shed dormer (Illus. 9-2). Some people call shed dormers "strip" dormers. Shed dormers are typically much larger than gable dormers; they're used to add floor space, with good headroom. Small shed dormers are often added to house a bathroom. Large shed dormers can run the length of the attic to expand the entire area. Illustrations 9-3 and 9-4 show two more views of shed dormers.

Installing either of these dormers will mean altering the existing roof. If you have a truss roof, don't try to cut in a dormer. As you learned earlier, engineered trusses are not meant to be cut. If you have a stick-built roof, dormers are viable options.

Building a Gable Dormer

First, locate where you want your dormer. Make sure the ground around your work area is clear of property and people that may be damaged or hurt by falling objects. Remove the roof covering from the area to be occupied by the dormer. Remove the roof sheathing once the shingles are out of the way, but don't cut the rafters yet.

Before you cut out the rafter sections, place temporary bracing under the parts of the rafters that will be left. This means putting a brace down low, near the top plate of the house, and up high, a little above where the rafters will be cut. Build your braces from 2 × 4s in the same way you'd prefab a wall section. Slide the braces under the rafters and tack them in place with nails.

Before cutting the rafter sections, add additional rafters at the edges of where your rough opening will be. Double up the rafters

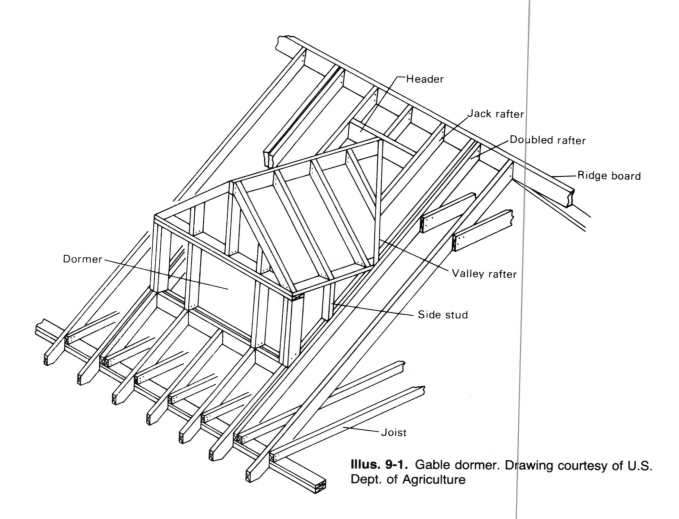

Header

Jack rafter

Doubled rafter

Ridge board

Dormer

Valley rafter

Side stud

Joist

Illus. 9-1. Gable dormer. Drawing courtesy of U.S. Dept. of Agriculture

Illus. 9-2. Shed dormer

Illus. 9-3 and **Illus. .9-4.** Two more views of shed dormers

Illus. 9-5. Valley rafters. Drawing courtesy of U.S. Dept. of Agriculture

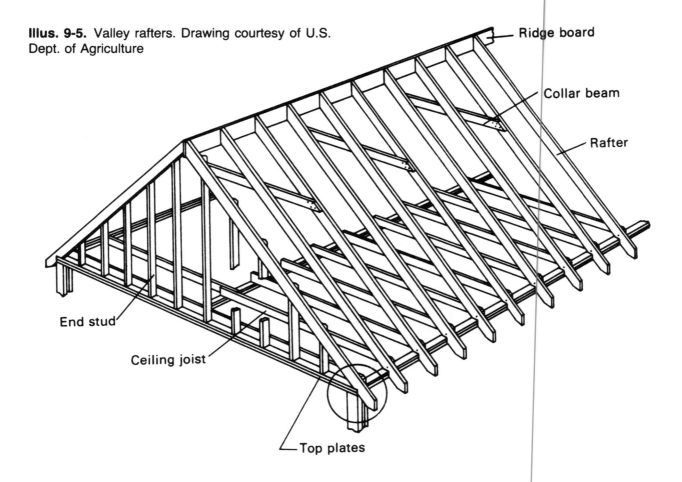

Ridge board

Collar beam

Rafter

End stud

Ceiling joist

Top plates

on each side of the proposed opening. The new rafters should extend from the top plate of the house to the ridge board.

Now remove the rafter sections (Illus. 9-5). When you cut out the rafter sections, be careful not to let them drop and damage the ceiling below the attic, or the side of the house. Cut them at an angle that will accommodate the new dormer. A bevel gauge can help to determine the desired angle. Once the rafters are cut out, you're ready to install the headers.

With this type of dormer, the lower portion of the original rafters will remain; this is where you'll put the first header. The header will span across from the two doubled rafters and attach to the lower rafter sections that are left. Use metal joist hangers (Illus. 9-6) to attach the rafter sections to the header. Once this header is complete, install another header near the ridge pole. This header will span from the two jack

rafters and it will butt against the middle rafter that you cut.

Once the headers are installed, the remainder of the job is just basic framing. The side studs for the dormer will rest on the doubled rafters. Run a ridge board from the front of the dormer to the header you installed near the main ridge board. The ridge board will be supported on the outside end by a stud rising from a double top plate in the new dormer. The two valley rafters will run from the doubled rafters to the new header you installed near the main ridge board. The jack rafters will connect with the valley rafters (Illus. 9-7) and tie in.

The front studs of the dormer will rest on the lower header and extend to the dormer's top plate. The dormer's top plate will attach to the front and side studs. The front gable end of the dormer will be filled in with studs connecting from a double top plate to the dormer's roof rafters and ridge board. The

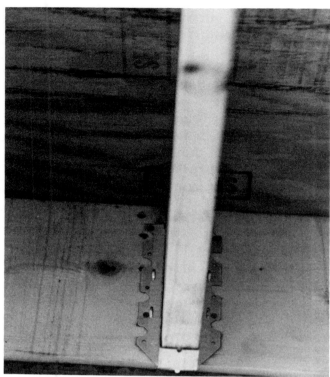

Illus. 9-6. Metal joist hanger

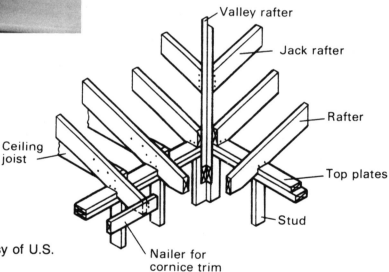

Illus. 9-7. Valley rafters. Drawing courtesy of U.S. Dept. of Agriculture

roof of the dormer will be framed with rafters extending from the top plate to the ridge board.

Framing a Shed Dormer

Framing a shed dormer can be a much bigger job than building a small gable dormer, since you'll affect much more of the existing roof structure, and the size of the project can be considerably larger. Framing a shed dormer is described below.

Opening the Roof

Opening the roof for a shed dormer will be done in nearly the same way as was done with a gable dormer. The only major difference will be that the only rafter sections left will be those attached to the ridge board.

Instead of leaving short sections of rafters sitting on the top plate, as you do with gable dormers, you remove the entire section, so that the new dormer can sit on the house's top plate. When planning the roof hole, don't cut too close to the gable ends on the roof. You will want some of the rafters and sheathing to remain on each end. Once the roof is opened, you'll be ready to begin framing.

Heading Off the Severed Rafters

Start framing by heading off the severed rafters. The header should span the dormer opening and attach to the doubled rafters.

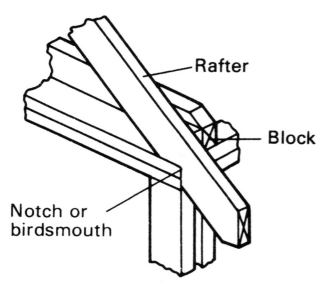

Illus. 9-8. Notched rafters. Drawing courtesy of U.S. Dept. of Agriculture

Once the header is in, frame the dormer walls. The front wall of the dormer is framed like any other wall. It sits on the top plate of the house, and its top plate will accept the new rafters for the shed dormer. Remember to brace this wall so that it doesn't fall off the house. The braces can swing back into the attic and be nailed to blocks attached to the attic's subfloor.

Now install the new dormer roof rafters. One end of the rafters will attach to the header with joist hangers. The other end will be notched (Illus. 9-8) to rest on the top plate of the new dormer. Start by cutting a single rafter. Once you have one rafter with the proper notch and angle, use it as a template for cutting the remaining rafters. Install the rafters. Where the rafters rest on the top plate, toenail them in (Illus. 9-9).

Now install the side-wall studs. The bottom plate for these studs will rest on the existing roof sheathing. Cut the bottom plate and nail it to the existing roof and doubled rafters. Once the plate is secure, cut the side-wall studs.

The side-wall studs will normally be notched with an L-shaped notch at the top. This notch allows the stud to cradle the end rafter. Since the bottom plate is installed on a slope, the bottom of the side-wall studs will have angled cuts. The studs will get progressively shorter as they move from the front of the dormer to the back. Nail the studs to the bottom plate and to the end rafters. When this is done, your framing will be complete.

Closing In the Dormer

After the framing is done, close in the dormer. The roofing methods described in chapter 4 can be used to install the roof sheathing and shingles. The walls should be covered with some type of sheathing. Some builders use plywood for wall sheathing and others use particleboard. Many carpenters use a foam insulation board for sheathing, and some use fibreboard sheathing.

Local codes will probably require wood sheathing (or the use of corner braces) on the corners in the absence of wood sheathing. The type of sheathing used will depend upon your preference and local customs.

Install the windows before you put siding on the new dormer. Whether you used a gable dormer or a shed dormer (Illus. 9-10), you could add a sewing room, a bedroom, or a family room there. Color plates T, U, and V show some ideas for dormer conversions.

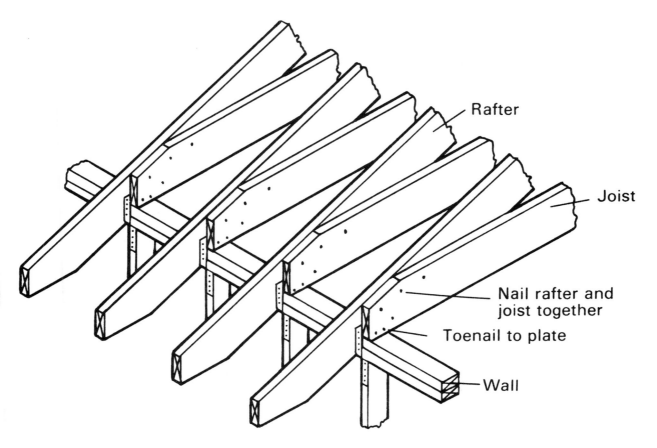

Illus. 9-9. Toenailing rafter. Drawing courtesy of U.S. Dept. of Agriculture

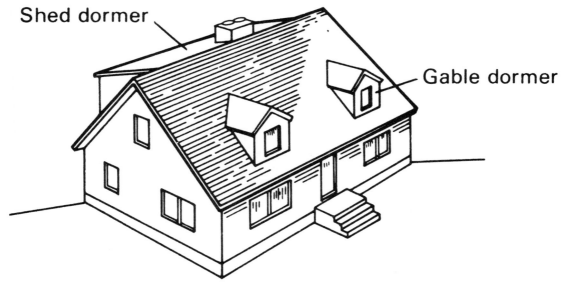

Illus. 9-10. Dormer examples. Drawing courtesy of U.S. Dept. of Agriculture

10
Exterior Siding Alterations & Trim

If you add a dormer or raise the roof, you'll have to make alterations and additions to the existing exterior siding and trim. Compared to building the dormer or raising the roof, this job will seem easy.

Types of Siding

There are several different types of siding: wood, vinyl, hardboard, and aluminum. The sidings used most often in modern building techniques are wood and vinyl. Some types of siding are installed horizontally and others are installed vertically. Most siding comes in widths of either 4″ or 8″. Some types of siding come in 4′ × 8′ sheets. Siding is generally sold in quantities called "squares." One square is equal to 100 square feet.

Exterior Trim Components

Exterior trim consists of fascia boards and soffits (Illus. 10-1). The soffit is the trim you see when you look up, under the overhang. The fascia board is the piece that conceals the tails of the rafters. Some homes have *frieze boards*. Frieze boards are the trim boards that are installed at the top of the siding, where the siding meets the soffit. *Rake boards* are boards on the gable ends that run parallel to the roof slope and trim the side of the house.

Different Installation Methods

There are many ways to install siding. Vinyl siding is typically installed horizontally. This durable siding is installed with the use of special installation pieces, and each piece of siding overlaps and locks into the previous piece of siding. Wood clapboards are thick at the top and narrow at the bottom. This wood siding laps over the previous piece of siding and nails to the exterior wall. Clapboards are also installed horizontally.

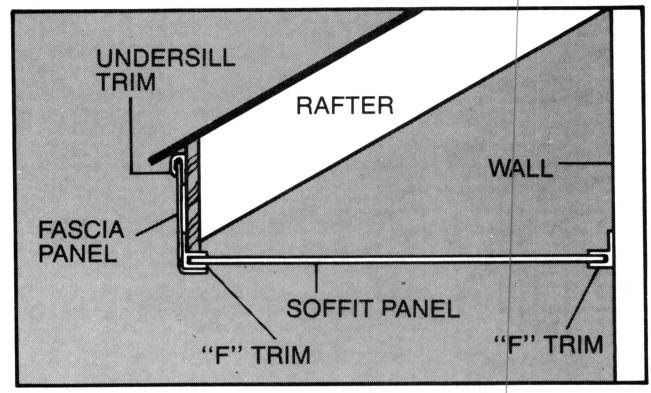

Illus. 10-1. Exterior trim detail. Drawing courtesy of Georgia-Pacific Corp.

The siding that comes in large, 4′ × 8′ panels, is normally installed vertically. These panels butt to each other and are nailed to the exterior walls. The seams of these panels are covered by a device like a tongue and groove on the siding. Wide siding planks are sometimes installed vertically; the planks butt together, and the seam is covered with a small vertical trim board.

Some wood siding comes in long lengths and is used as tongue-and-groove. Siding shakes are small, individual pieces of siding that are lapped over each other to cover the exterior of the house.

Working with Wood Clapboards

When you add siding to cover new framing, matching the old siding and color can be the hardest part of the job. You could try to match the new with the old as closely as possible, or you could make the new siding different, so that it doesn't look like a failed attempt to match the old siding. If you're siding a small dormer, the dormer is high enough and far enough away from the old siding that a minor mismatch won't be apparent.

In most traditional homes, changing either the pattern or the type of siding won't look good. Contemporary homes allow more freedom for changes in direction and styles of siding. In conversion projects, new siding can almost always be separated from old siding. Dormers are naturally separated. When raising the roof, the new siding will be on the gable ends. Creative use of trim boards can provide separation for this siding.

Most wood clapboards are pine or cedar. If you don't know which type of siding you have, take a small sample to your lumber supplier for an evaluation. By using the same species of wood, you can do a good job with custom-mixed paint or stain to match existing siding, even if the original siding has weathered.

Siding Nails

Choose siding nails carefully. Nails that are too large will split the siding. The wrong nails will rust and send dark stains running down the exterior of new siding. The proper nails will usually be either aluminum, stainless steel, or galvanized steel.

Which Side Out?

Wood siding has a rough side and a smooth side. If you'll be painting the siding, install it with the smooth side exposed. When you plan to stain your siding, expose the rough side. Stain will soak into the rough side much better than it will the smooth side, for good deep coverage.

Corner Boards

Corner boards will be needed on the corners of your framing. These wood strips are installed vertically and give the siding a place to end. Corner boards are normally of 1″ material. They're installed on each wall at the corner and they butt together. Interior corners are made by installing a vertical square wooden strip.

Hanging the Siding

Hanging the siding requires some planning. All window flashing (and all other flashing) should be installed before the siding is applied. The average lap for wood siding should be no less than 1″. A starter strip is nailed at the bottom of the wall to be sided. Local codes will normally require a minimum clearance between the siding and the earth.

The thick end of the siding is the bottom. The first piece of siding is placed on the starter strip and nailed in place. Then, the

Illus. 10-2. Newly installed vinyl siding

next piece of siding is set over the previously installed piece and nailed into place. The siding nails should be going into wall studs. Many carpenters mark the exterior walls with chalk lines to keep the siding even and attractive. Without the chalk lines, the siding may stray and end up mismatched.

Avoid butt seams. When seams must be made in long runs, stagger them. Staggered seams are much more attractive than a uniform line running up the side of your home. Seams should be made at stud locations so that the end of each piece of siding can be nailed to the stud.

Vinyl Siding

Vinyl siding is very popular; it's durable and it never needs painting. Due to its nature, vinyl siding expands and contracts. This expansion and contraction require special installation methods. If the siding isn't installed properly, the expansion and contraction can damage it. Some newly installed siding is shown in Illus. 10-2.

Nails

The nails used to install vinyl siding should be either galvanized steel or aluminum roof-

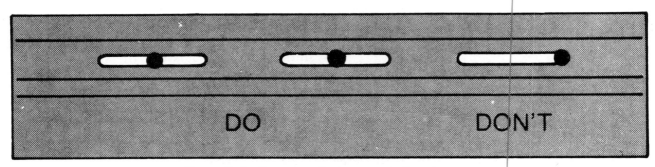

Illus. 10-3. Proper nail placement. Drawing courtesy of Georgia-Pacific Corp.

Illus. 10-4. Proper nailing procedure. Drawing courtesy of Georgia-Pacific Corp.

Illus. 10-5. Improper nailing procedure. Drawing courtesy of Georgia-Pacific Corp.

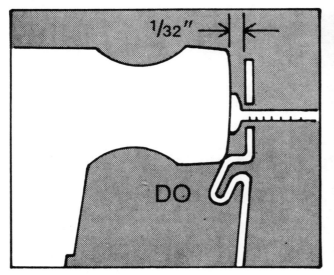

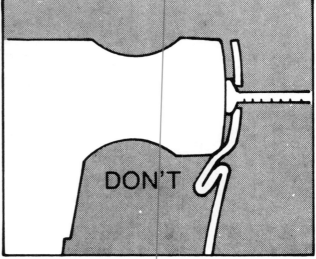

Illus. 10-6. Starter strip. Drawing courtesy of Georgia-Pacific Corp.

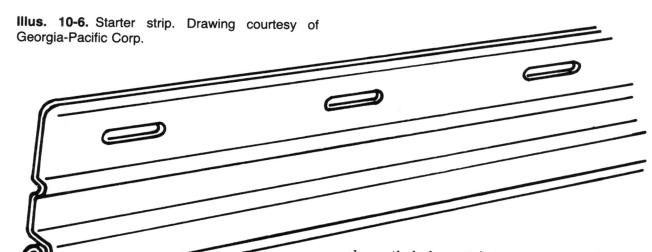

ing nails. The head of the nail should be about ⅜". Each nail's shank should have a diameter of about ⅛". The length of the nail will be determined by the thickness of the material to be nailed through. The nails should be long enough to penetrate at least ¾" into a stud.

Never nail into the face of vinyl siding. The siding will have a nailing strip where

the nails belong. It's important to place the nails in the middle of the nailing slot. If the nail is too far to one side of the slot, expansion and contraction will be restricted (Illus. 10-3). If the nailing slot doesn't line up with a stud, extend the size of the slot. A special tool, called a nail-slot punch, can be used to extend the nailing slot.

When nails are driven into the nail slots, a small gap should be left between the nail head and the slot. If the nail is driven tightly into the slot, expansion and contraction can cause problems. All nails should be driven in straight. If the nail enters at an angle, it

Illus. 10-7. Installation of starter strip. Drawing courtesy of Georgia-Pacific Corp.

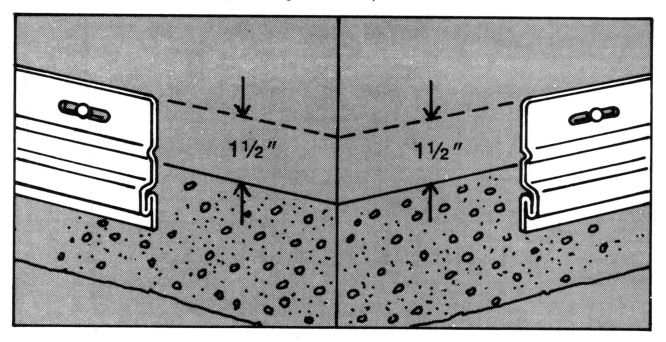

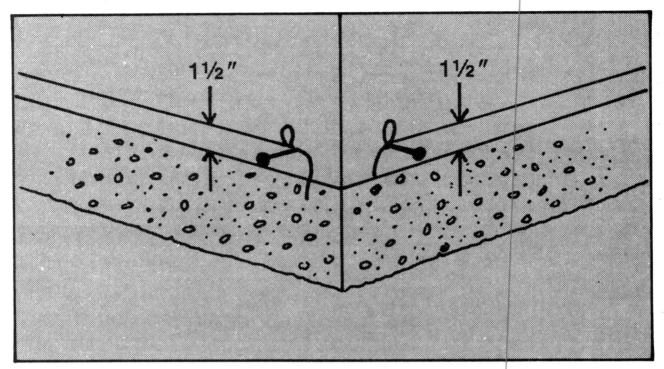

Illus. 10-8. Chalk line. Drawing courtesy of Georgia-Pacific Corp.

can cause stress on the siding (Illus. 10-4 and Illus. 10-5). Vinyl siding should never be stretched to fit. If the siding is too tight, problems will arise.

Starter Strips

Starter strips (Illus. 10-6) are accessory pieces used to hang vinyl siding. These strips will be installed at the lowest point on the area to be sided (Illus. 10-7). The top of the starter strip will normally be about 1½″ above the bottom of the wall sheathing. These starter strips must be level. Normally, a chalk line is used to mark a level line on the wall sheathing. The chalk line (Illus. 10-8) is used as a reference point when installing the starter strips.

When starter strips butt together, there should be a ¼″ gap between the strips (Illus. 10-9). This gap allows the siding to expand and contract. The same nailing techniques used for vinyl siding should be used for accessory pieces.

Corners

Inside (Illus. 10-10) and outside (Illus. 10-

11) corners are made with corner posts. These posts are installed vertically and extend about ¼″ below the starter strips. Inside and outside corner posts can be overlapped (Illus. 10-12) when additional length is needed. This requires cutting about 1″ off the bottom of the top post. Then, the top post can slide down over the lower post to meld together. The overlap of the post should be about ¾″, with ¼″ allowed for expansion and contraction.

J-Channel

J-channel (Illus. 10-13) is an accessory piece that's used around windows and doors, and in other places, to give the vinyl siding something to attach to (Illustrations 10-14 through 10-17). It's usual to wrap J-channel all the way around windows to achieve a "finished" look. When doing this, another accessory piece called an undersill (Illus. 10-18) is used for a good-looking job.

Cutting Vinyl Siding

Cutting vinyl siding isn't difficult. You could use a power saw with a fine-tooth blade (Il-

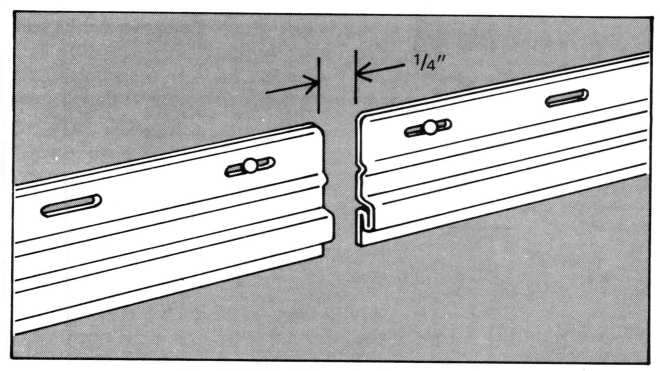

Illus. 10-9. Butting starter strips. Drawing courtesy of Georgia-Pacific Corp.

Illus. 10-10. Inside corner. Drawing courtesy of Georgia-Pacific Corp.

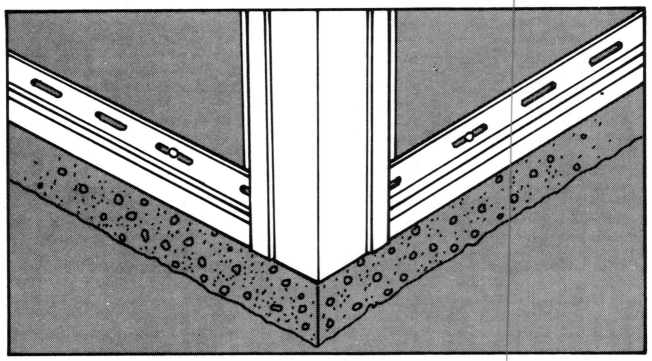

Illus. 10-11. Outside corner. Drawing courtesy of Georgia-Pacific Corp.

Illus. 10-12. Splicing corner posts. Drawing courtesy of Georgia-Pacific Corp.

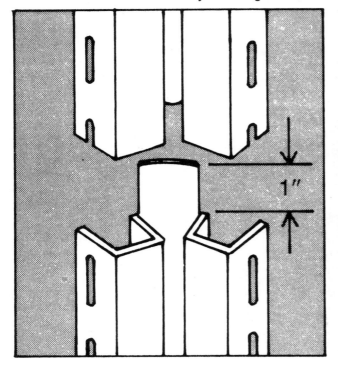

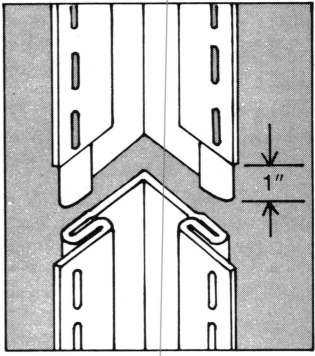

Basement game room. Photo courtesy of Georgia-Pacific Corp.

Basement family room. Photo courtesy of Georgia-
Pacific Corp.

Skylights. Photo courtesy of Velux-America, Inc.

Roof windows. Photo courtesy of Velux-America, Inc.

Roof windows with blinds. Photo courtesy of Velux-
America, Inc.

Cleaning a tilting roof window. Photo courtesy of
Velux-America, Inc.

Roof window in a bathroom. Photo courtesy of
Velux-America, Inc.

Bedroom roof window. Photo courtesy of Velux-America, Inc.

Cutaway of a skylight. Photo courtesy of Velux-America, Inc.

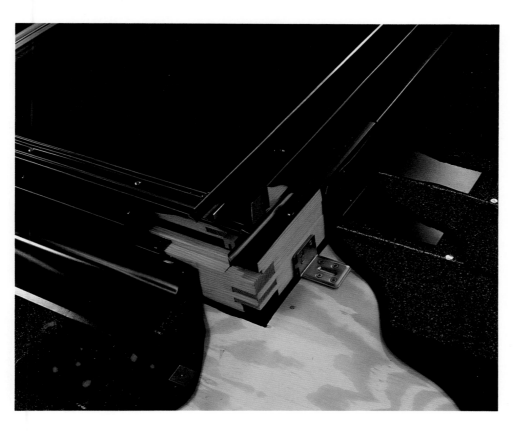

Bedroom roof windows. Photo courtesy of Velux-America, Inc.

House with roof windows. Photo courtesy of Velux-America, Inc.

Sewing room. Photo courtesy of Ralph Wilson Plastics Co.

Bedroom. Photo courtesy of Ralph Wilson Plastics Co.

U

Family room. Photo courtesy of Ralph Wilson Plastics Co.

Installing drywall. Photo courtesy of Georgia-Pacific Corp.

Faced insulation being installed. Photo courtesy of
Georgia-Pacific Corp.

Illus. 10-13. J-channel

lus. 10-19), or you could use a hacksaw (Illus. 10-20). Aviation (tin) snips will also work well (Illus. 10-21).

Hanging the Siding

Hanging the siding is simple. Starting at one corner, usually a rear corner, snap the bottom of the siding into the starter strip (Illus. 10-22). When the siding is seated in the starter strip, nail the siding to the wall studs. The siding should be held away from the corner posts by about ¼″.

Illus. 10-14. J-channel installation. Drawing courtesy of Georgia-Pacific Corp.

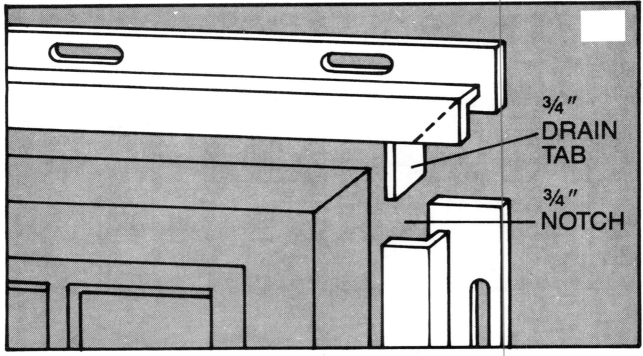

Illus. 10-15. J-channel installation. Drawing courtesy of Georgia-Pacific Corp.

Illus. 10-16. J-channel installation. Drawing courtesy of Georgia-Pacific Corp.

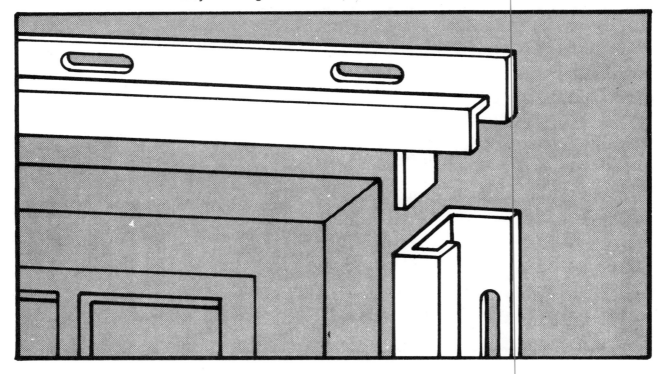

Illus. 10-17. J-channel installation. Drawing courtesy of Georgia-Pacific Corp.

When two pieces of siding butt together, the overlap should be between 1″ and 1¼″ (Illus. 10-23). Where these overlaps occur, nails should be at least 10″ away from the overlap. This distance will make a neat job. Overlaps should be staggered (Illus. 10-24) to avoid seams on the face of the house.

Getting to the Top
When you get to the top of the wall, install undersill strips (Illus. 10-25). These finish strips will be installed horizontally, where the wall meets the roof. The last piece of siding to be installed will generally have to be cut. This means cutting off the nailing flange. With the nailing flange gone, you'll use a snap-lock punch to attach the siding.

Once the top piece of siding is cut, use a snap-lock punch to dimple the siding (Illus. 10-26). The dimples should be about 6″ apart, and they should be raised on the outside of the siding. When you're done punching the siding, install the bottom of the siding just as you have been doing all along.

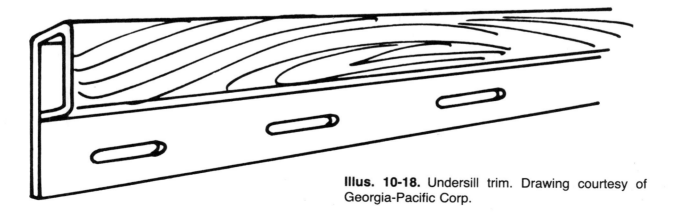

Illus. 10-18. Undersill trim. Drawing courtesy of Georgia-Pacific Corp.

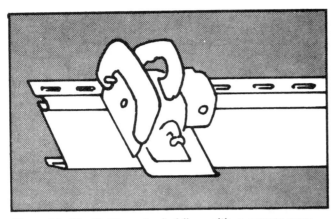

Illus. 10-19. Cutting vinyl siding with a power saw. Drawing courtesy of Georgia-Pacific Corp.

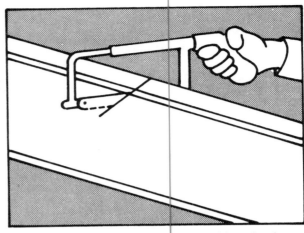

Illus. 10-20. Cutting vinyl siding with a hacksaw. Drawing courtesy of Georgia-Pacific Corp.

Illus. 10-21. Cutting vinyl siding with tin snips. Drawing courtesy of Georgia-Pacific Corp.

Now, instead of nailing the top of the siding, push the dimpled siding into the undersill trim (Illus. 10-27). The raised bumps will catch and hold the siding in place.

Gable Ends

Gable ends are finished off with J-channel, which is run with the slope of the roof (Illus. 10-28). The siding is cut with the proper angle (Illus. 10-29) to allow it to fit into the J-channel, which provides a finished surface and trim to hide the cut edges of the siding (Illus. 10-30).

Helpful Hints

It's not uncommon for bees to take up residence behind siding. Bats have been known to fly out from behind old siding as it was being removed. When you're up on a ladder and bees or bats suddenly fly out from behind the siding you can lose your composure and your balance.

Always wear the proper safety equipment. Never drop items to the ground without making sure that the area below is clear of people and pets.

Illus. 10-22. Installing the first piece of siding. Drawing courtesy of Georgia-Pacific Corp.

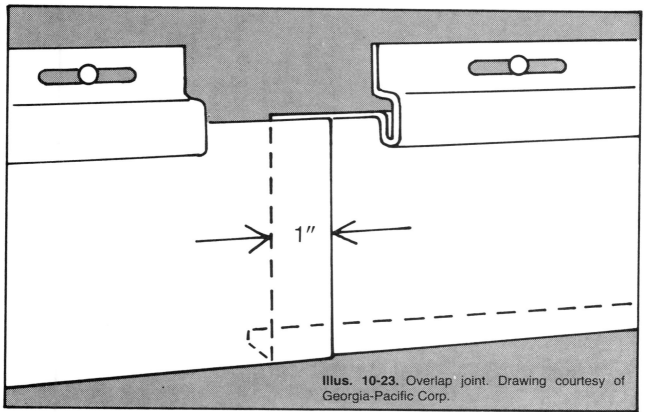

Illus. 10-23. Overlap joint. Drawing courtesy of Georgia-Pacific Corp.

Illus. 10-24. Stagger panels. Drawing courtesy of Georgia-Pacific Corp.

Illus. 10-25. Undersill trim in place. Drawing courtesy of Georgia-Pacific Corp.

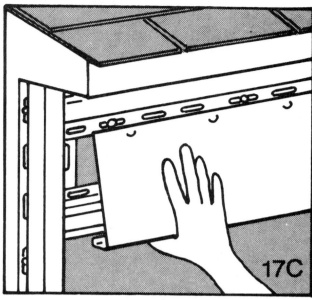

Illus. 10-26. Dimple siding. Drawing courtesy of Georgia-Pacific Corp.

Illus. 10-27. Installing dimpled siding. Drawing courtesy of Georgia-Pacific Corp.

Illus. 10-28. J-channel on gable end. Drawing courtesy of Georgia-Pacific Corp.

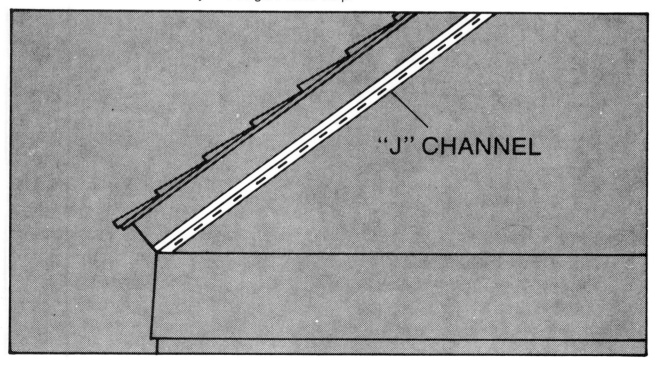

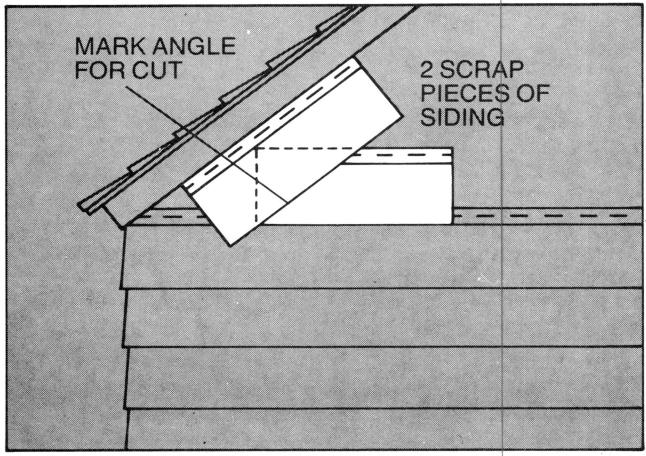

Illus. 10-29. J-channel cut. Drawing courtesy of Georgia-Pacific Corp.

Illus. 10-30. Finished gable. Drawing courtesy of Georgia-Pacific Corp.

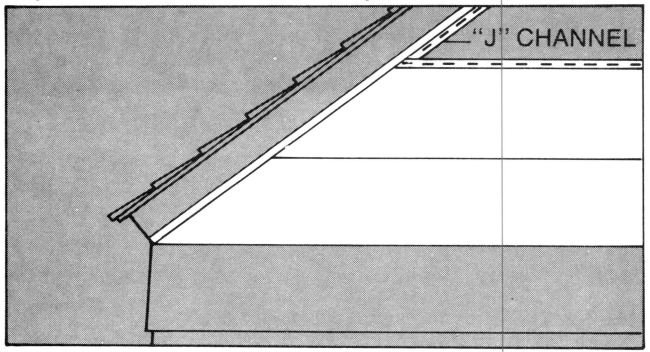

11
Plumbing Rough-In

Plumbing is the one area of construction work that many people fear, due largely to a poor understanding of how plumbing works. For most residential conversions, plumbing is basic and fairly simple. Many times the hardest part of the job is finding a way to get new plumbing to the space being remodelled.

Types of Drain-and-Vent Pipe

There are many types of drain-and-vent pipe, but there are only a few that you are likely to work with.

Cast-Iron Pipe

Cast-iron pipe has long been the standard for plumbing. This durable pipe has been used for drains and vents for many years, and it's still used today. If you'll be remodelling an older home, it's very likely that you'll have to work with some cast-iron pipe. You may have to connect your new piping to old cast-iron pipes.

In the old days, cast-iron pipe joints were made with oakum and molten lead. Today, special rubber adapters are used to make connections with cast iron. These adapters slide over the ends of two pipes and are held in place with stainless-steel clamps. This type of connection is easy to make, and it's safer than working with hot lead.

Cutting cast-iron pipe can be easy or it can be torture, depending upon how well you do it. If you'll be cutting cast-iron pipe, consider renting a ratchet-type soil-pipe cutter. This handy device has a chain that wraps around the pipe. When the chain is in place, crank up and down on the handle of the tool. In a matter of moments, the cast iron is cut. Most tool-rental centers rent these cutters at very affordable rates.

Caution: If you're cutting a vertical cast-iron pipe, take some extra safety precautions. Cast iron is heavy. When you cut a section out of a vertical pipe, the pipe over your head might come crashing down. Always support any pipe section that might fall on you. You can support these sections with wood braces or with perforated galvanized strapping.

Galvanized Steel Pipe

Galvanized steel pipe, another "old-timer," isn't installed much anymore, but there's

Illus. 11-1. Soldered copper pipe

Illus. 11-2. Close-up view of the solder

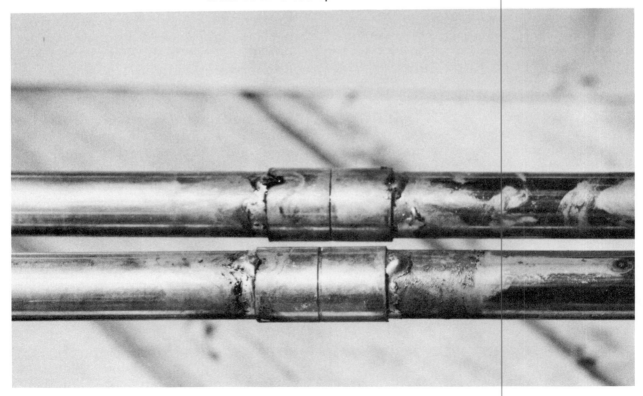

Illus. 11-3. Plastic waste pipe

Illus. 11-4. Close-up view of plastic drain pipe

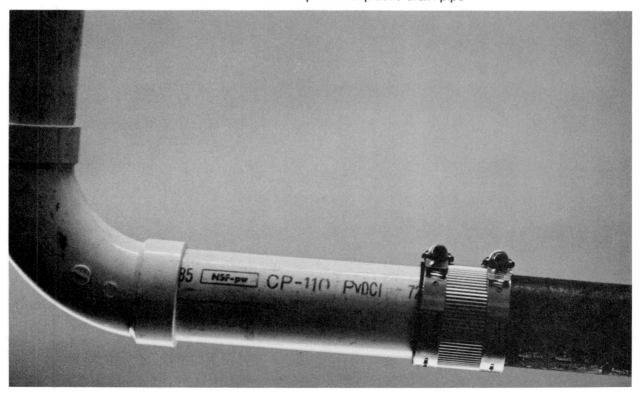

still plenty of it around. If you have to make a connection with galvanized pipe, the cut can be made with a hacksaw. The joint can be made with the same rubber adapters used with cast-iron pipe.

DWV Copper

DWV copper can still be found as a drain-waste-and-vent (DWV) pipe in older homes. This good DWV pipe enjoys a long life. When you need to adapt plastic pipe to copper, you can do so with rubber adapters. DWV copper can be cut with a hacksaw, but a set of copper roller-cutters will do a neater job. Either tool will cut the pipe satisfactorily for use with rubber adapters. Illustrations 11-1 and 11-2 show copper pipes. Illustrations 11-3 and 11-4 show plastic pipes.

Schedule-Forty Plastic Pipe

Schedule-forty plastic pipe is the drain-and-vent pipe most often used in modern plumbing systems. There are two types of schedule-forty plastic pipe: ABS and PVC.

ABS is a black plastic pipe that's easy to cut either with a hacksaw or a handsaw, and it's a breeze to work with. PVC, a white plastic, can also be cut with either a hacksaw or a handsaw, but it cuts a little harder than ABS. PVC becomes brittle in cold weather, so don't drop cold PVC pipe on a concrete floor, since the pipe will likely crack.

When you work with these plastic pipes, joints are made with solvent or glue. With PVC, a cleaner is recommended and a primer is required by most plumbing codes. The cleaner and primer are used prior to gluing the joints together. These types of pipe can be connected to cast-iron or galvanized-steel pipe by using the universal rubber adapters.

Types of Water Pipe

Many types of water pipe are available. Some are easier to work with than others; some require soldering, others are glued together.

Illus. 11-5. Roller cutters

Copper

Copper water pipe and copper tubing are longtime favorites. Copper pipe is best cut with roller-type cutters (Illus. 11-5), but it can be cut with a hacksaw. The biggest drawback to copper is that it must be soldered (Illus. 11-6). Since many homeowners don't know how to solder, they often opt for a plastic water pipe.

Even when you use a different type of pipe for new plumbing, you may still have to connect to existing copper pipe. This can be done even if you can't solder. Compression fittings can be used to make the transition from copper to the new pipe material. Threaded fittings and adapters can also be used in some circumstances.

CPVC Pipe

Most professional plumbers don't use CPVC pipe. Compared to other pipe materials, this pipe is slow and finicky to install. However, many homeowners find CPVC to be an ideal choice for water pipe.

CPVC, a plastic pipe, can be cut with a hacksaw, and it also glues together. A cleaner and primer should be used on the joints before they're glued together. Don't move fresh joints, since it takes time for them to cure. If CPVC is moved before the joint sets, leaks will occur.

Polybutylene Pipe

Polybutylene (PB) pipe is becoming very popular with professional plumbers. This plastic pipe is very flexible and easy to install with the proper tools. It uses insert fittings and special crimp rings to make its joints. The tools needed to make these joints can often be rented. The pipe can be cut with a hacksaw.

Due to its flexibility, polybutylene can be snaked through walls, much like electrical wiring. Since it is available in long coils, the pipe can be run with a minimum of concealed joints, giving polybutylene pipe another advantage. For attic conversions, where pipe must be snaked up, PB is a good

Illus. 11-6. Soldering copper pipe

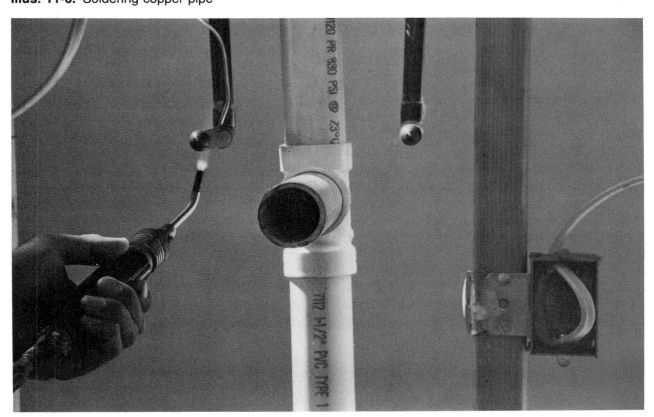

Illus. 11-7. Rough-in for a toilet connection

choice. If you decide to use PB, make sure that you have the proper tools and that you follow the manufacturer's installation procedures.

Common Rough-In Dimensions

Here are some common rough-in dimensions for various residential plumbing fixtures: The drain for a lavatory should be roughed in at the center of the lavatory and at about 17″ above the subfloor. The water pipes for a lavatory will rough in on 4″ centers, about 2″ on either side of the drain, and about 21″ above the subfloor.

The drain for a common toilet will rough in at 12½″ out and away from the back stud wall. When measuring from the center of the toilet drain to either side, there should be a minimum of 15″ of clear space. This means the closet flange should have at least 15″ from its center to any finished side wall or fixture. The water supply for a toilet is roughed in 6″ to the left of the center of the drain and about 6″ above the subfloor. Illustrations 11-7 and 11-9 show some roughed-in toilet plumbing.

A bathtub drain will typically be located 15″ off the stud wall where the back of the tub will rest. The drain will normally be about 4″ off the head wall, where the faucets go. When roughing in a tub hole, most plumbers cut the hole to extend from the head wall to a point about 12″ away and about 8″ wide, making a hole that's 8″ wide and 12″ long. You'll need most of this space to connect a tub waste and overflow (Illus. 11-8) to the tub.

If you'll be installing a faucet for a tub, the faucet is usually set about 12″ above the flood-level rim of the tub. The flood-level rim is the arm rest (or such a location) where

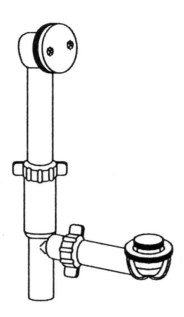

Illus. 11-8. Tub waste and overflow. Drawing courtesy of Moen Inc.

Illus. 11-9. Another view of a toilet water-supply pipe

water will first spill over the tub. The tub spout is normally mounted about 4″ above the flood-level rim of the tub.

When you install the faucet for a shower, the faucet is ordinarily set about 4′ above the subfloor. The shower-head outlet should be installed about 6′6″ above the subfloor.

The drains for a kitchen sink will be between 15″ and 18″ above the subfloor. The water-supply openings for a kitchen sink are normally roughed in about 21″ above the subfloor.

A washing machine hookup will have a standpipe that rises between 18″ and 30″ above its trap. The water supplies will be set at a height of 4′ to 5′ above the floor.

With all fixtures that use hot water, hot water should be piped to the left side of the fixture and cold water should be piped to the right side.

All of these dimensions are "averages," and they'll vary with local plumbing codes and with specific product manufacturers. Check product information and local codes before installing your plumbing.

Basement Plumbing

Basement plumbing can present its own set of challenges. The existing drains may be too high to allow new fixtures to drain by gravity. It can be quite difficult to get a vent pipe from the basement to the roof. The concrete floor might need to be broken up in order to install plumbing.

How can I find the drains under the floor?

One way to find drains under the floor is to look for clean-out caps. These screw-in caps are installed to allow access for cleaning the drain lines, and they provide a visible means of locating some pipes. You could start breaking up the floor at the base of plumbing stacks entering the floor. This way is effective, but it can cause undue damage to the floor. If your drains are made from cast iron, a good metal detector can be used to trace the direction of under-floor drains. *There aren't any drains under the floor. What can I do?*

If you're installing a toilet, you'll have to install a sewer ejector or a specialty toilet. Some toilets are designed to flush up, others incinerate waste. If you're only installing a sink, like that for a wet bar, you may be able to tie into an existing waste pipe before it exits the foundation. If all the pipes are above drainage level, you'll have to install a pump.

Installing a sewer ejector isn't a complicated job, but it does require a bit of labor. The concrete floor must be broken up. You can rent electric jackhammers that will do an efficient job on residential floors. Then, a pit must be dug to accept the sewer sump. Once the sump, a watertight container, is set in place, run the plumbing beneath the floor. The plumbing fixtures drain into the sump. When the waste level rises to a certain point, a sewer pump will turn itself on and pump the waste out of the house.

The sewer pump will plug into a normal household electrical outlet. The sump will have a gasket-sealed top and will be vented to the outside air, to prevent odors and sewer gas from entering the basement. The drain pipe from the pump will have a check valve to keep the waste in the vertical piping from running back into the sump. There will be a gate valve installed on the drainage line to facilitate repairs and maintenance on the pump.

The concrete floor will have to be filled in and patched. The filling-in is usually done with sand. The patching is usually done with a sand mix, similar to concrete but without the rocks. The sand mix will give a smooth finish.

How do I vent my plumbing?

Under most plumbing codes, each plumbing fixture must have a vent. The most com-

mon way to vent a plumbing fixture is with an individual vent that runs to a vent stack or to outside air. Vents must rise at least 6" above the flood-level rim of a fixture before being run horizontally.

In some cases, a benevolent plumbing inspector may allow the use of a mechanical vent. These vents screw into 1½" female adapters and provide air for a fixture to drain better. In remodelling jobs, these vents are sometimes allowed instead of running a vent all the way to the roof. However, if you'll be installing a toilet or a sewer sump, plan on running a 2" vent to the outside air or to an approved connection point with another vent.

When you have to get a vent from the basement to the attic, look for closets to run the vent in. Consider building a small box-chase in a corner to allow the installation of the pipe. The routing of the vent from a basement is often the hardest part of the job.

Can I run my vent up the outside of my house?

Some plumbing codes do allow sidewall vents. These vents must be protected from freezing, in cold climates, and they mustn't terminate under a soffit vent. There are restrictions pertaining to the proximity of the vent to windows, doors, and even to property boundaries. Check with your local code officer for details on sidewall vents.

My drain goes out at floor level. What can I do?

If you position your bathroom or plumbing near the existing drain, you may be able to build up the new floor with a sleeper system to allow height for your new drains. Check the ceiling-height requirements before raising the finished floor level.

Can I tie into the pipe for my floor drain?

Most floor drains will be connected to a pipe of at least 2" in diameter. In fact, the minimum pipe size for pipes running under concrete is usually 2". The floor drain could be connected to a 3" or 4" drain.

As long as you can vent the new fixtures, there shouldn't be any problem with tying into the same pipe used by the floor drain. The local plumbing code does set requirements for the number of fixtures placed on a pipe, so check code requirements before making such a connection.

Can I cut a tee into that vertical pipe for my lavatory?

The odds are good that you can. The pipe must have a minimum diameter of 1¼″, but almost any plumbing pipe you encounter will be at least this large.

Can I tie into my kitchen sink's water pipes?

It depends on how many fixtures you will be tying into the pipes and how many fixtures are already served by the pipes. As a rule of thumb, don't serve more than two plumbing fixtures with a single ½″ water line. If the pipes have a ¾″ diameter, you should be fine.

Attic Plumbing

Attic plumbing can be very different from basement plumbing. Gravity drainage isn't a problem, nor is access to vents. However, getting water pipes into the attic can require some thought.

Can I use that big vertical pipe for a drain?

That big vertical pipe extending through the attic is a main vent. Normally, it would be acceptable to tie into this pipe for a drain. However, as with all plumbing, check the local code first.

How can I get plumbing up to my attic?

You may have to open existing walls from below. It's possible to build chases for the pipes to run up, putting them in closets. In some cases, it may be possible to snake pipes up through existing partitions. If the walls aren't filled with fire-blocking or wiring, it's often possible to get pipes up without opening the walls.

Since my attic plumbing is so high up, does it need a vent?

Yes. All plumbing fixtures should be vented.

How can I get a bathtub into my attic?

One-piece bathtubs can't be carried up most stairways. If you plan to use a one-piece tub, put it in while you're framing the dormer or attic openings. If this is impossible, opt for a standard bathtub and a fibreglass or tile shower surround.

Garage Plumbing

Garage plumbing can be difficult, since the plumbing may be too far from existing drains, or the grade of the pipes may not allow connection. Getting water pipes to the garage can also be a problem.

I want a bathroom in my garage. What should I do with the drain?

It may be possible to intersect your home's sewer at some point in the lawn. If this is impossible, you'll have to run a separate sewer for the garage plumbing.

How will I get new plumbing in my garage?

You'll generally have to break up a section (a corner, usually) of the concrete floor. Then, a hole is dug to allow pipes to come in beneath the garage's footing. All pipes coming through or under a wall should pass through a protective sleeve, which should be at least two pipe-sizes larger than the pipes passing through.

When running water pipes to my garage, how deep should they be?

The depth for buried water pipes will depend on the local climate. Your local plumbing code will provide information on the minimum depth.

How much can I cut out of my floor joists for plumbing?

Most building codes require a minimum of 2″ to be left at the top and bottom of floor joists. If more than this is notched or cut, steel plates or headers are usually required.

How often should I support my horizontal pipes?

The distance between supports will be determined by local plumbing codes and by the type of pipe being installed. In general, plan on support intervals of 4′ for drain and vent pipes and 6′ for water pipes.

Inspections

Plumbing is a logical trade. With common sense and the right tools, plumbing isn't difficult. There are rules to be followed, and you'll normally need to apply for a permit to do your work. Most jurisdictions require up to four inspections. If you'll be running a new sewer or water service, such work will need to be inspected. Any plumbing installed underground or under a floor will need to be inspected before the trench is covered or the floor is poured. All plumbing that will be concealed in walls should be inspected prior to concealment. After you set your fixtures a final inspection is usual.

Before doing your own plumbing, check with the local code-enforcement office for current rules and regulations. Always be sure to turn off the water running to any pipes you'll be cutting. Avoid contact with the contents of waste and soil pipes. If you're unsure of yourself, call in a professional. Illus. 11-10 shows some professional-quality plumber's wrenches.

Illus. 11-10. These wrenches are essential tools for the experienced plumber

12
Electrical Rough-In

Electrical wiring is not hard to understand, but working with electricity can be very dangerous. Unlike plumbing, where a mistake is likely only to get you wet, a mistake with electricity can be fatal. Electricity shouldn't be feared, but it should be respected.

When you convert an attic, garage, or basement to living space, you'll have to make alterations in the electrical system. You might have to increase the size of the main service panel. You may only have to run a few new circuits or install a ground-fault interceptor, but count on making changes.

Upgrading the Service Panel

Upgrading the service panel is a job that's best left to qualified professionals. This job involves working around high voltage, and the risk of a fatal injury is always present. Unless you're a licensed electrician, don't attempt to change your entrance panel. *When will the service panel need to be upgraded?*

Service panels have different ratings, depending upon their size and how they're set up. In old houses the main electrical panel may be a 60-amp fuse box. These fuse boxes usually have two large, boxlike fuses and a few small screw-in-type fuses. See Illus. 12-1.

Most modern houses will have circuit breakers in the main service panel. These breaker boxes will usually be rated for either 100 or 200 amps. See Illus. 12-2. If your box is set up for 200 amps, it's unlikely that you'll need to upgrade the panel.

With a 60-amp fuse box, it would be wise to upgrade to a higher-capacity circuit-breaker system. If you have a 100-amp service panel and you will be adding electrical heat in your converted space, you will want to upgrade to a 200-amp box.

Adding a Subpanel

Adding a subpanel can be a big help when wiring for an attic or garage conversion. A subpanel is a small service panel that connects to the main service panel. The subpanel

Illus. 12-1. A fuse box

could contain fuses or circuit breakers, but circuit breakers are preferable.

If you don't install a subpanel, each circuit in your newly converted space will have to have a wire that runs back to the main service panel. By installing a subpanel in or near the new space, you can reduce the amount of wire used and the number of wires returning to the main service panel. Of course, the subpanel will be an additional expense, but there is also the convenience and safety of having the panel close at hand.

Selecting a Box

Selecting an electrical box is important. Depending upon the type of installation you are roughing in for, you will need the right box for the job. Some of the options are described below.

Rectangular Boxes
Rectangular boxes are commonly used for switches, wall outlets, and wall-mounted

Illus. 12-2. The main service panel

Illus. 12-3. Rectangular box

lights (Illus. 12-3). The dimensions for rectangular boxes are generally 3″ × 2″.

Octagonal Boxes
Octagonal boxes are most frequently used for ceiling lights. They may also be used as junction boxes, to join numerous wires together. These boxes are typically 4″ along each edge.

Round Boxes
Round boxes are used primarily for ceiling lights.

Square Boxes
Square boxes are most often used as junction boxes. Square boxes have a typical dimension ranging from 4″ to just over 4½″.

Box Depth
The depth of electrical boxes varies from 1¼″ to a full 3½″. Depth plays an important role in determining how many connections the box may hold. For example, a 3″ × 2″ switch box with a depth of 2½″ can accommodate six connections with a number 14 wire. The same box, but with a depth of 3½″ could hold nine connections. Ground wires usually count as a connection.

Means of Attachment
The ways to attach different boxes will vary, but some ways are easier than others. One of the easiest, and most common, boxes used in modern jobs is the plastic box with nails already inserted. These plastic boxes are nailed directly to wall studs. The boxes are sold with nails already inserted in a nailing sleeve. All you have to do is position the box and drive the nail.

Illus. 12-4. Metal box with nailing ear

Some metal boxes are set up with a nailing flange that resembles an ear (Illus. 12-4). To attach these boxes, position the box and drive nails through the flange and into the stud. This type of box is good because the flange allows for the thickness of common drywall.

Other metal boxes, usually meant for use in existing construction, are equipped with adjustable tabs. These tabs, or "ears," allow the box to be attached to plaster lathe, or any other material that will accept screws.

Octagonal and round boxes are often nailed directly to ceiling joists. If these boxes need to be offset, such as in the middle of a joist bay, metal bars can be used to support the boxes. The metal bars are adjustable and will mount between ceiling joists or studs (Illus. 12-5). Once the bar is in place, the box can be mounted to the bar.

Common Heights & Distances

Wall switches are usually mounted about 4' above the finished floor. Wall outlets are normally set between 12" and 18" above the floor. Most codes require wall outlets to be spaced so that there's no more than 12' between the outlets.

Wire Moulding

Wire moulding is a protective trim that's placed over wires when the wires are run on the outside of walls and ceilings. This moulding can be installed after the wiring is run. The wire moulding is hollow and open on the bottom, allowing it to be laid over existing wires. When you can't conceal your

Illus. 12-5. Housing mounted between joists

wires in a conventional way, wire moulding should be used to protect yourself and the wiring.

Conduit

Conduit is another way of running wires when conventional methods can't be used. Wires must be pulled through the conduit. Conduit can't be installed over existing wires. The conduit acts as a protective tunnel for the wires.

Snaking Wires

"Snaking" (pulling) wires through a wall is done using a "fish tape," a thin, flexible, metal tape on a spool (Illus. 12-6). The exposed end of the tape has a hook on it. Some people simply bend the wire to be fished over the hook on the fish tape. Electricians usually bend the wires over the hook and then tape them, to ensure that they don't come loose.

Fish tapes can be used to get wires up and down wall cavities. However, fire-blocking in the walls can block fish tape. Fire blocks are staggered blocks of wood nailed between the wall studs. These wood blocks help to impede airflow and prevent the wall cavities from acting as chimneys during a fire. If you find fire-blocking in the wall, the wall must be opened.

Fish tapes are often worked from around outlet boxes. By removing the cover of an outlet box, you have access to the interior of the wall. For example, if you needed a wire in your attic, you could drill a hole in the wall plate. Then, from below, you could remove an outlet cover as a second opening for working the fish tape. Between these two openings, you could fish a wire up or down the wall, to either opening.

Color Codes

Color codes are common in wiring. For example, a black or red wire is usually a "hot" wire. A white wire *should* be a neutral wire,

Illus. 12-6. Fish tape

but these wires *could* be hot. Green wires and plain copper wires are typically ground wires. Here's how to match these colored wires to the various screws in an electrical connection: Black wires should connect to brass screws. Red wires should connect to brass or chrome screws. White wires will normally connect to chrome screws. Green wires and plain copper wires should connect to green screws.

Putting Wire Under the Screw

When you put wire under a screw, the wire should be bent to tighten as the screw is tightened (Illus. 12-7). If you hook the wire in the opposite direction, it may come loose. Always twist the hook in the end of the wire to match the clockwise tightening of the screw (Illus. 12-8).

Wire Nuts

Wire nuts are available in different sizes and colors (Illus. 12-9). The colors indicate the size of the wire nuts. Wire nuts are plastic on the outside and have wire springs on the inside. When wires are inserted into the wire nut, the nut can be turned clockwise to secure the wires. It may be necessary to twist the wires together before installing the wire nut. It's important to use a wire nut of the proper size. Wire nuts should be installed to a depth where no exposed wiring is visible (Illus. 12-10).

Split Circuits

Split circuits are frequently used in kitchens and in rooms where switch-operated table lights are used. In a split circuit, one half of an outlet remains hot at all times, usually the top half of the outlet. The bottom half of

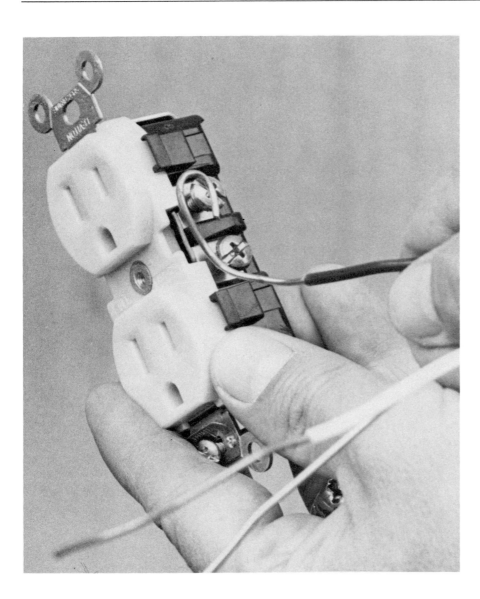

the outlet is controlled by a switch. Split circuits are frequently used in the kitchen to avoid overloading a single circuit. In kitchens, it's not uncommon for both halves of the outlet to remain hot, but on separate circuits.

Ground Fault Interrupters

Ground fault interrupters (GFIs), sometimes called ground fault *interceptors*, ground fault *breakers*, or ground fault *outlets* (Illus. 12-11)

are usually required anywhere water may come into contact with an electrical outlet. Bathrooms in particular are generally required to be equipped with a GFI. Outdoor receptacles normally require GFIs.

There are two common ways to provide GFI protection. First, you could install a GFI outlet. These outlets have a built-in test and reset button. It is recommended that GFIs be tested every month. The other manner of protection is a GFI breaker. This is a special circuit breaker that's installed in the service panel. Either of these devices will protect against accidental shocks in a wet area. GFIs

Illus. 12-8. Tightening the screw

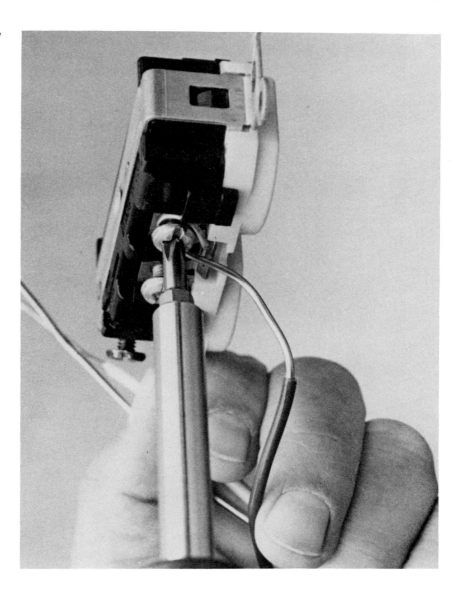

aren't cheap, but in most places they're a code requirement for wet-use areas, and they're an excellent safety feature.

High-Voltage Circuits

Appliances that use high voltage (such as a clothes dryer or an electric range) require their own high-voltage circuits. The outlets for these high-voltage circuits will use a plug with a different pattern from that of a standard wall outlet. Appliances that use these special plugs are often fitted with "pigtails,"

special wiring arrangements with high-voltage prongs that allow the appliance to be plugged into the high-voltage outlet. High-voltage circuits will run directly from the outlet to the service panel.

Floor Outlets

Floor outlets are generally frowned upon by electricians and electrical inspectors. When used, electrical outlets mounted in the floor should be equipped with waterproof covers. When possible, avoid installing floor outlets.

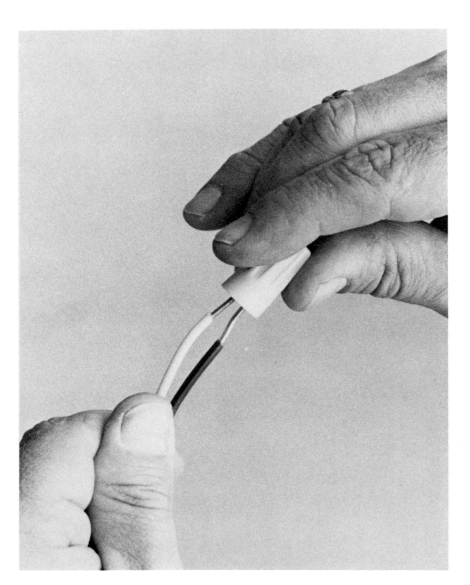

Illus. 12-9. Wire nut

Design Ideas

Ceiling lights aren't installed as often as they once were. However, a large portion of the population still likes the idea of having good light cast down from the ceiling. Don't hesitate to install ceiling lights if they suit you.

Track lighting is popular, and it can answer many lighting needs. Recessed lights can be attractive, but due to their recessed installation, they're limited in the illumination they can provide.

Install more outlets and switches than you think you'll need (Illus. 12-12). It's much easier to add extra electrical devices while the walls and ceilings are open than it is to add such devices after the walls are done.

Always apply for the proper permits and have the required inspections for electrical work. Improper wiring can result in electrical shocks and house fires.

If you hire an electrician, be sure that he's licensed and insured. You may even want your electrician to be bonded.

Illus. 12-10. Wire nut installation

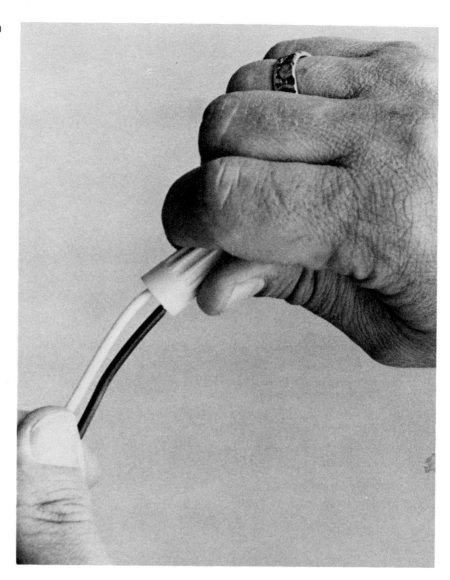

Making Final Connections

I believe that only qualified professionals should make the final connections for electrical wiring. The risk of working inside service boxes and subpanels is just too great for the average homeowner. A licensed electrician should inspect your work and make the final connections.

Illus. 12-11. GFI outlet

Illus. 12-12. Gang box

13
HVAC Rough-In

Climate control is a part of any successful remodelling conversion. Heating, ventilation, and air conditioning (HVAC) are all components of climate control. Some questions about HVAC include:

Will the existing system be capable of handling the additional load?

Should a separate zone be run from the boiler to heat the new space?

Would electric baseboard heat be a good choice?

Could a wood stove or oil-fired space heater save money?

Window Air Conditioners

If the climate warrants the use of air conditioning equipment, window air conditioners can be a good choice for converted living space. These independent units are affordable and easy to install. With window air conditioners, there's no need for additional ducts, and there's no extra strain on an existing central air conditioner.

Window units are especially practical when converting a garage. Since garages are usually located far from existing ducts, it's much easier to install window units than it is to add new ducts. The amount of livable square footage in a garage is small when compared to the space available in most houses. Because of a garage's smaller habitable space, window air conditioners are quite capable of cooling the area.

The effectiveness of window air conditioners will be determined, in part, by the design of the living space. If the space is divided into several rooms, a single window unit won't be satisfactory. If, however, the space is mostly open, one window unit can do an excellent job.

When converting an attic, more than one window unit will normally be required. Since many attic conversions consist of two bedrooms and a bathroom, it would be logical to install a window air conditioner in each bedroom.

Central Air Conditioning

Central air conditioning relies on ducts (Illus. 13-1) to convey cool air and to direct that cool air to all rooms. Central air condi-

Illus. 13-1. Air-conditioning ducts

tioning provides more uniform cooling than window air conditioners can provide.

If you plan to extend existing ducts to cool new space, you'll have to determine if the existing cooling unit is capable of handling the increased load. If the unit is large enough for the job, finding places to run the new ducts will be the next challenge. Ducts are frequently run through built-in chases. It is a simple matter to box in duct work in new construction, but with remodelling work, the task can be more trying.

Consider running new ducts up through closets. If you need the closet space, find an area that can be boxed in. Such areas are often *next* to closets. When the back wall of a closet extends into a room or hall, there will be a natural chase created by the wall jutting out. These spaces can be boxed in so that the box becomes an extension of the protruding wall.

Forced Hot-Air Heat

Forced hot-air heat is also conveyed through ducts. The same problems presented by central air conditioning will exist with forced hot-air heat. Getting the ducts to the desired locations is the biggest challenge.

When adding forced hot-air heat, keep the registers in the floors or low on the walls. Hot air rises, so the lower the registers are, the more heat you'll keep in the room. Heat registers should be placed along exterior walls, normally around windows.

When using forced hot-air heat, cold-air return ducts should be installed. The number of returns will depend upon the size and design of the converted space. Install a cold-air return in every large room. The cold-air returns allow cool air to be returned to the furnace for reheating.

Example of good window selection. Photo courtesy of Andersen Window Corporation, Inc.

Example of good door selection. Photo courtesy of Andersen Window Corporation, Inc.

Wall of windows in the attic bedroom. Photo courtesy of Andersen Window Corporation, Inc.

Pedestal lavatory. Photo courtesy of Ralph Wilson
Plastics Co.

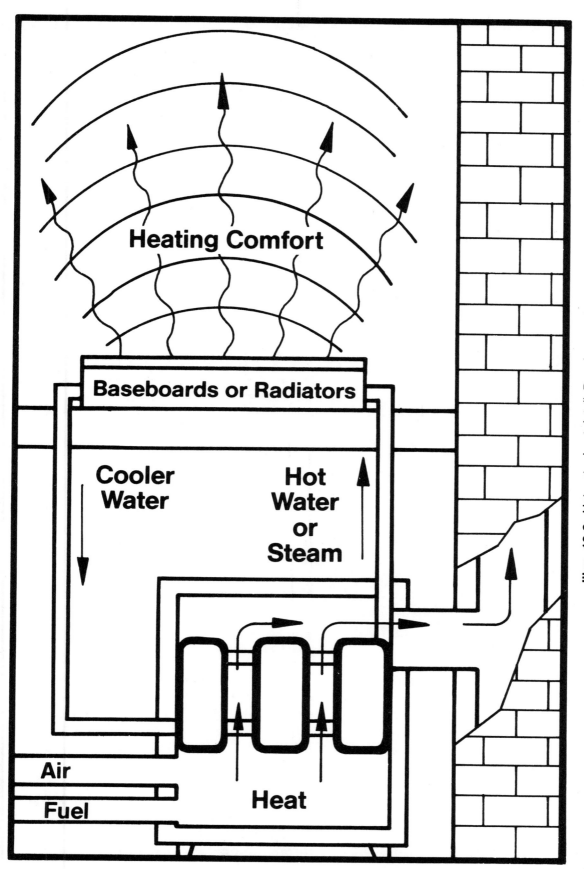

Heating Comfort

Baseboards or Radiators

Cooler Water

Hot Water or Steam

Heat

Air

Fuel

Illus. 13-2. Hot water heat detail. Drawing courtesy Weil-McLain/A Division of The Marley Company

Illus. 13-3. Detail of a hot-water boiler

One of the drawbacks of a forced hot-air heating system is dust. Since the system works by blowing warm air, dust is moved along with the air. For some, this dust can be uncomfortable. If you're sensitive to dust, consider a different type of heating.

Heat Pumps

Heat pumps provide heating and air conditioning from a single unit. There are two basic styles of heat pump. The first type is a through-the-wall heat pump. These units resemble window air conditioners because they're installed through an exterior wall, with part of the unit inside the home and the other end outside. The other type of heat pump has two main parts: an indoor part and an outdoor part. The outdoor part stays outside and is connected to the inside part through piping.

Illus. 13-4. Close-up view of part of a hot-water boiler

Heat pumps are not very efficient for heating when the outside temperature is below freezing. However, most heat pumps are equipped with a type of back-up electric heat to compensate for lower temperatures. While this electric heating will overcome some of the heat pump's deficiency, it is an expensive way to heat your home. Heat pumps are ideal in parts of the country where there is a high air conditioning demand and a low heat demand.

Forced Hot-Water Heat

Forced hot-water heat is popular in cold climates because it produces steady heat that can tame the coldest winters. Most modern forced hot-water systems use copper tubing and baseboard heating units. The baseboard heating units contain copper tubing (normally with a ¾″ diameter) that's surrounded by metallic fins. Hot water is forced through the copper tubing in the baseboard heating

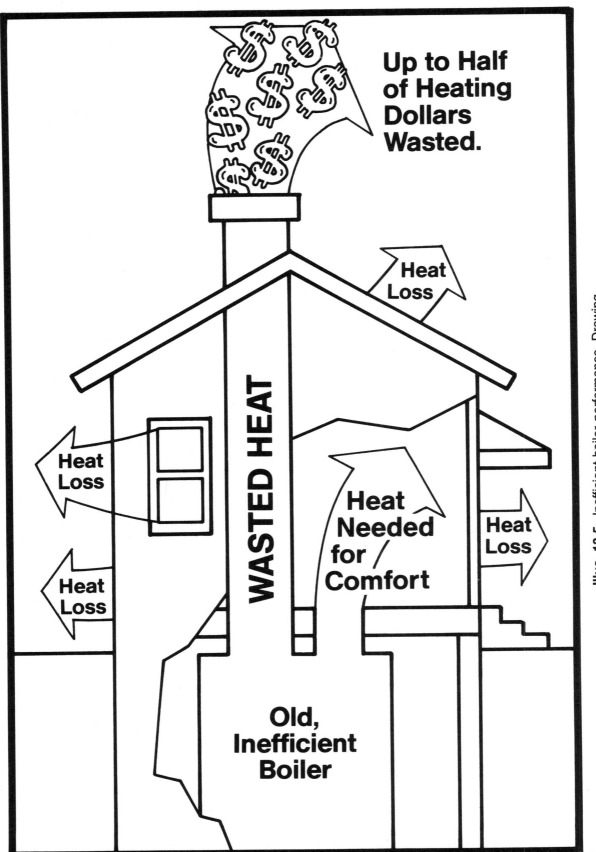

Illus. 13-5. Inefficient boiler performance. Drawing courtesy Weil-McLain/A Division of The Marley Company

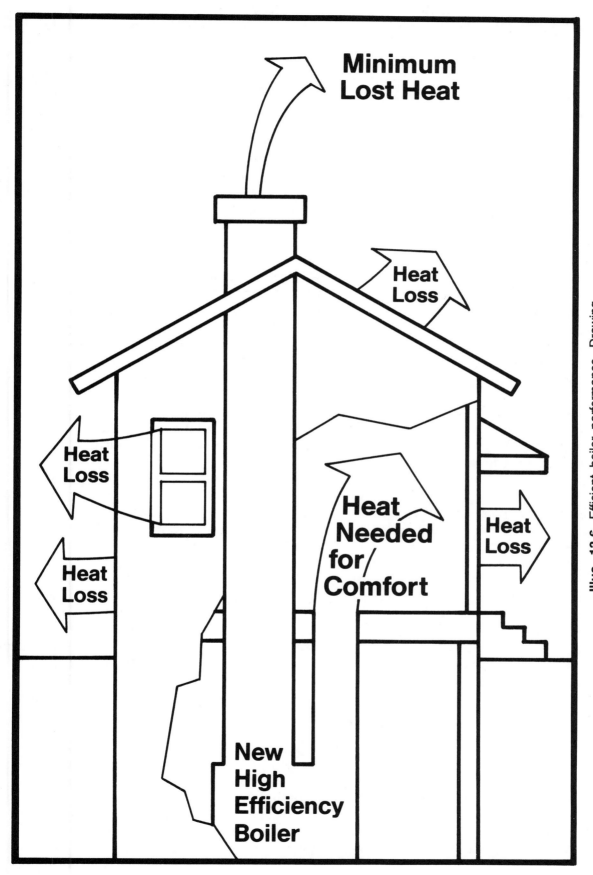

Illus. 13-6. Efficient boiler performance. Drawing courtesy Weil-McLain/A Division of The Marley Company

units. Heat is gathered in the fins and radiated into the living space.

This type of heating system depends on a boiler to generate hot water. The boiler produces hot (around 180 °F) water and a circulating pump forces the water around the heating circuit (Illus. 13-2). It's possible to install multiple zone valves or circulating pumps to create different heating zones. Each zone can be controlled by its own thermostat. Having individual zones makes it more economical to heat a home. Zones serving rooms that aren't in use can be turned down, while the heat in active zones can be turned up.

If the existing boiler has the capacity to handle new heating demands, new zones can be added to serve newly converted living space. Illustrations 13-3 and 13-4 show details of new hot-water boilers. If your existing boiler is old (Illus. 13-5), it might be wise to replace it with something more efficient (Illus. 13-6). These systems can be installed either as one-pipe systems or two-pipe systems. With a one-pipe system, the supply pipe starts at the boiler and makes a continuous loop through the heated area and back to the return side of the boiler. With a two-pipe system, one pipe supplies hot water to the heating units and a second pipe carries the used cooled water back to the boiler.

A one-pipe system is cheaper to install, but it's also less efficient. The water in a one-pipe system cools as it travels through the pipes and heating units. By the time the last heating unit receives its water, the water can be much cooler than it was when it entered the first heating unit. A two-pipe system provides more stable heat, because cooled water is returned in one pipe while hot water is supplied in another.

Steam Heat

Steam heat and radiators are found in some older homes. Such systems generally work on a gravity principle, without need of a pump. The piping for a steam system can consist of one or two main pipes. In a one-

pipe system, steam rises up the pipe to radiators. As the steam gives off heat, it turns to condensate and runs back down the pipe, and then to the boiler. With a two-pipe system, the steam rises to the radiators in one pipe and the condensate returns to the boiler in another.

Steam-heating systems don't respond quickly to temperature changes. This fact alone is enough to warrant the consideration of a different heating system for your converted space. Further, steam-heating systems can be noisy.

Electric Heat

Electric heat can be a good choice for heating converted living space. Operating electric heat can be expensive, but there are times when electric heat can be a reasonable choice.

Adding ducts or heat pipes to an attic or a garage can be a major chore. Electric heat is easy to install and it provides adequate heat, although it is expensive to operate. Consider how often you'll be heating your new space. The money you save by installing electric heat might go a long way to heating it. Before installing electric heat, be sure your electrical panel is large enough. You will probably need a 200 amp panel to run electric heat.

Electric heat comes in many forms. Baseboard heating units are most common, but electric heat can also be purchased as a radiant wall heater (Illus. 13-7), a fan-forced heater (Illus. 13-8), a register heater (Illus. 13-9), a kickspace heater (Illus. 13-10), or a high-wattage wall heater (Illus. 13-11).

Hot air rises, and an attic will be warmer than the lower floors of a home. If you remove the insulation from the attic floor, the heat from below will rise to warm the attic. Something as simple as cutting a floor register into the attic floor could do wonders for your heating needs. You could cut in floor grates at each end of the attic. These grates will allow even more heat to pass from downstairs to the converted attic.

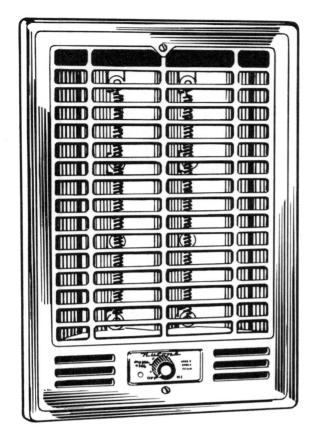

Illus. 13-7. Electric radiant wall heater. Drawing printed wth permission of NuTone Inc.

Illus. 13-8. Fan-forced electric heater. Drawing printed wth permission of NuTone Inc.

Illus. 13-9. Electric register heater. Drawing printed with permission of NuTone Inc.

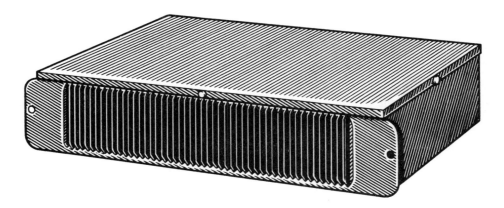

Illus. 13-10. Electric kickspace heater. Drawing printed with permission of NuTone Inc.

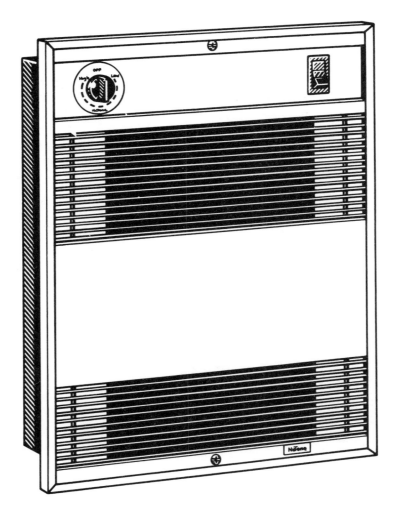

Illus. 13-11. Electric high-wattage heater. Drawing printed with permission of NuTone Inc.

Wood Stoves

Wood stoves can add both charm and warmth to a room. Combining a wood stove with electric heat is a popular option in some regions. The wood stove provides the bulk of needed heat, and the electric heat provides backup heat and heat for those times when the room is unattended.

A flue or chimney will be required for a wood-stove installation. Most fire codes limit the use of a flue to one connection. Some areas might allow two connections to a common flue, but check local building requirements before tapping into an existing flue. Even if you're allowed to put two connections on a common flue, it isn't a good idea. The use of a common flue for multiple connections can lead to excessive soot and creosote buildup. The risk of a chimney fire is increased when more than one connection is made to a common flue. There's also a risk of dangerous gases accumulating (due to poor draft) in an overloaded flue. This accumulation can lead to fire or asphyxiation.

Installing a new flue in an attic is fairly easy. A triple-wall stovepipe can be run from the stove to a point above the roof. When installing this metal pipe, follow the manufacturer's installation instructions. When the stovepipe passes through wood, use an approved flange collar to support the pipe and to maintain proper distances from combustible materials. Avoid horizontal stovepipe installations. If you must run stovepipe horizontally, keep the horizontal runs as short as possible.

When picking a spot for your stove, place it at least 3' from any combustible material. Even if a wall has a heat shield, maintain a safe distance from it. The stove should rest on a fireproof base. This base could be masonry, heavy tile, or stone.

Installing a wood stove in a basement can be more difficult because of the need to run the chimney. There are two options for installing a metal chimney for a basement wood stove. First, you could use triple-wall, insulated stovepipe and run it up through the living space of the house until you exit the roof. You'll most likely want to box in the chimney. This can be done, but maintain minimum distances between the chimney and combustible materials.

The second option is to extend the chimney up the outside of the house. The stovepipe rises from the stove and then turns horizontally to exit the basement. When the pipe penetrates the exterior wall, a special adapter should be used to allow it to penetrate the wall without risk of fire. Then, with the use of a wall bracket, the chimney turns to a vertical position and extends past the roof. Stand-off clamps will be installed along the chimney to hold it to the house. By installing the chimney in this fashion, you won't disturb the upstairs living space.

Local building codes will influence the installation of your wood stove and chimney (Illus. 13-12). Chimneys must extend well above the roof (Illus. 13-13). Local codes will dictate the precise measurements for these extensions. Check local code requirements before doing your work.

Ceiling fans can do much to improve heating and cooling circulation. These fans are available with or without light kits (Illus. 13-14 and Illus. 13-15). If you have a vaulted ceiling, a ceiling fan is attractive and helpful. If your upstairs will incorporate a loft, a fan with a reversible motor can help maintain a comfortable temperature.

Space Heaters

Space heaters are available in many styles and types. The three most common types are electric, kerosene, and gas-fired. Space heaters can provide supplemental heat or even primary heat.

Kerosene heaters require good ventilation. High-quality kerosene heaters are designed to be vented to the outside. These units can be thermostatically controlled and provide good heat. Portable kerosene heaters don't have outside vents. Such heaters can pose a serious (if not fatal) health risk.

Many gas-fired space heaters are designed for a direct vent through an outside wall.

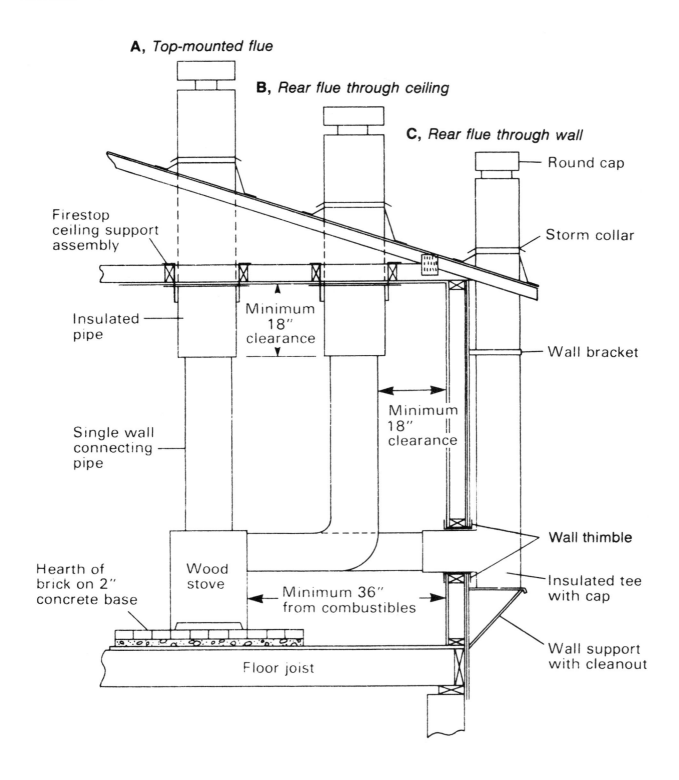

A, *Top-mounted flue*

B, *Rear flue through ceiling*

C, *Rear flue through wall*

Round cap

Firestop ceiling support assembly

Storm collar

Insulated pipe

Minimum 18" clearance

Wall bracket

Single wall connecting pipe

Minimum 18" clearance

Hearth of brick on 2" concrete base

Wood stove

Minimum 36" from combustibles

Wall thimble

Insulated tee with cap

Floor joist

Wall support with cleanout

Illus. 13-12. Flue installation methods. Drawing courtesy of U.S. Dept. of Agriculture

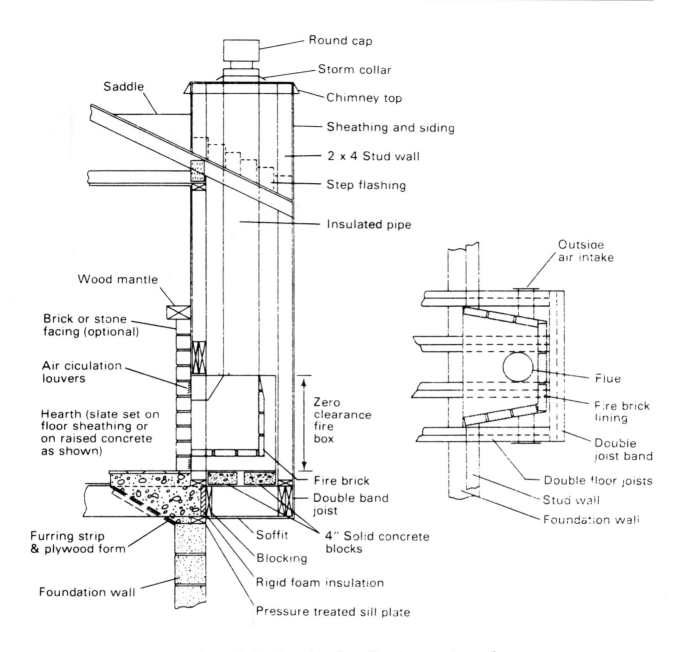

Illus. 13-13. Boxed-in flue. Drawing courtesy of U.S. Dept. of Agriculture

These heaters, when properly installed, can provide warmth and comfort, with easy installation.

Electric space heaters don't require a vent. Two possible concerns with this type of heater are the risk of contact burns (also a concern with other types of space heater), and an electrical-system overload. Most electric heaters put a heavy demand on electrical wiring. If your wiring is inadequate, a fire could occur. Before using an electric space heater, be sure the wiring is sized and fused properly.

If you'll be adding a bathroom that won't have a window, you'll need a ventilation fan for the bathroom. These fans mount in the ceiling (Illus. 13-16) and they move stale air to the outside. Many such fans are available with a built-in light (Illus. 13-17).

Illus. 13-14. Ceiling fan without light. Drawing printed with permission of NuTone Inc.

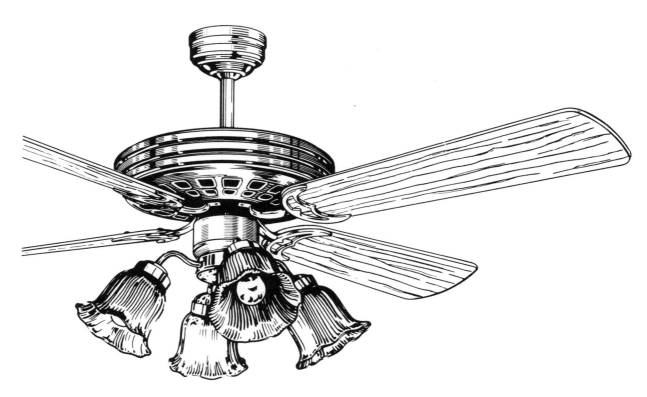

Illus. 13-15. Ceiling fan with light. Drawing printed with permission of NuTone Inc.

Illus. 13-16. Ventilation fan for a bathroom

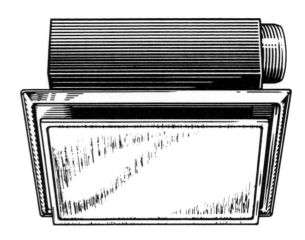

Illus. 13-17. Bath fan with a light. Drawing printed with permission of NuTone Inc.

14
Insulation & Drywall

When you get to insulation and drywall, your remodelling job is about half done. Most people then think that the worst is behind them, but there's still plenty to do, and much that could go wrong.

Types of Insulation

There are several types of insulation to choose from. Described below are the most common types of insulation and their uses.

Batt Insulation

Batt insulation is probably the most common form of insulation. These batts can consist of glass fibres or mineral wool. Glass-fibre batts are the most common. These rolls of batt insulation are available in various thicknesses and R-values.

Batt (or blanket) insulation is usually available in widths of either 16″ or 24″. The 16″ batts are used between wall studs, and the 24″ batts are used between ceiling joists. The thickness of this insulation will usually be (approximately) either 3″, 6″, or 9″. Thickness determines R-value. For example, a 3″

batt has an R-value of 11. A 6″ batt has an R-value of 19.

Batt insulation is available either faced or unfaced. The facing is either a foil or paper backing, and it provides a vapor barrier. The color section has one photo that shows such insulation. Insulation installed in walls is usually faced, while insulation in attic floors is usually unfaced. Batt insulation is commonly stapled to wood studs and joists.

Loose-Fill Insulation

Loose-fill insulation comes in bags and is meant to be either spread over or blown into an area. The material may consist of cellulose, glass fibre, mineral wool, perlite, or vermiculite. This is the type of insulation frequently blown into existing walls and attics. You can rent machines to blow this insulation into your new attic space. If you buy enough insulation, some stores will loan you the machine with which you'll blow in the insulation.

Foam Insulation

Liquid-foam insulation can be injected into existing walls with a special machine, but there is little need for it in attic, basement, and garage conversions.

Board Insulation

Rigid board insulation can be used in many ways. It can be installed on a roof to increase the insulating value, or it could be installed on basement walls for the same purpose. These rigid boards are sometimes installed below ground, on the outside of basement walls. Foam panels can be used as exterior wall sheathing to increase a home's R-value.

Rigid insulation boards are generally available in widths of 16", 24", and 48". The thickness of these boards can range from a mere ½" to a full 7".

Rigid insulation can be made from polystyrene or urethane or glass fibre. The polystyrene and urethane insulate better than the glass fibre. Install a vapor barrier with polystyrene and urethane boards. Without this vapor barrier, the boards can lose up to half of their R-value to moisture. Board insulation is normally nailed or glued into place.

Insulation Materials

There are many types of insulation material to choose from. What follows below is a description of the most often used materials and their benefits and drawbacks.

Glass Fibre

Glass fibre insulation can make people itch. Breathing the glass fibres that fly through the air during installation can be hazardous. This insulation is relatively inexpensive, and it's easy, although itchy, to install. Glass fibre is good because it tends not to settle, creating voids. It's also durable, resists most water damage, and is a low fire risk.

Cellulose

Cellulose is the insulation preferred by recyclers because it's made from recycled paper. This insulation is inexpensive and easy to install. However, if cellulose gets wet, it loses much of its insulating value. Untreated, cellulose presents a high fire risk. If you install cellulose, be sure it has been treated for fire resistance.

Mineral Wool

Mineral wool is somewhat similar to glass-fibre insulation. Take precautions with a mask, gloves, and full body protection when installing it. Like glass fibre, mineral wool can cause irritating reactions in some.

Polystyrene

Polystyrene is used in rigid boards. This is an excellent insulator, but it's highly flammable.

Vermiculite

Vermiculite is used in loose-fill insulation. This insulator is nonflammable; it doesn't emit any harmful fumes or gases.

Perlite

Perlite, like vermiculite, is used in loose-fill insulation. Perlite is nonflammable; it doesn't emit any harmful fumes or gases.

Urethane

This insulator was once very popular in its foam form. It was used to insulate houses that had no insulation and walls (such as brick) that were difficult to insulate. As time passed, urethane was discovered to endanger health, and many cities restricted or banned its use.

Urethane is an extremely efficient insulator. However, it's flammable, and when it's burned, it gives off cyanide, a deadly gas.

Vapor Barrier

When insulation is installed in walls and crawl spaces, a vapor barrier should also be installed. If you're using a glass-fibre insulation, it can be purchased with a vapor barrier already installed. Another way to create a vapor barrier is to wrap plastic over the interior of outside walls.

When using faced insulation, the facing should be installed to face the heated side of the wall. The goal is to keep moisture from the house from entering the wall cavity. When moisture enters a wall cavity, rot can occur in walls with no insulation, and even in walls *with* insulation but lacking a vapor barrier.

When moisture enters the wall, it can attack wall sheathing, insulation, siding, studs, and wall plates. This moisture attack can go unseen for years, until major structural damage has occurred.

Proper ventilation is another key to a healthy house. Poor ventilation can result in rot or cracking paint. It can also increase the risk of dangerous odors and gases in a home. A house without good ventilation can harbor a buildup of radiation. Good ventilation is provided by foundation vents, soffit vents, and attic vents. It's important to control moisture through good ventilation.

Working with Drywall

Working with drywall requires some special skills. Hanging drywall is fairly simple, except for the sheer weight of the material. Finishing the drywall to get acceptable seams is quite another matter; there's an art to finishing drywall.

Drywall is the leader in modern wall covering materials. It's inexpensive and, when properly finished, it produces an attractive wall or ceiling. Many do-it-yourselfers are unaware of what's involved when working with the heavy gypsum board. The remainder of this chapter will show you how to hang and finish drywall.

Materials
The choices for drywall are numerous. There's fire-rated drywall for use in garages, where the garage shares a common wall or ceiling with habitable space. Moisture-resistant drywall, which is usually green, is available for use in places like bathrooms, where there's high humidity.

Gypsum board is available in various thicknesses: ⅜", ½", and ⅝". The overall dimensions for wallboard can be 4' × 8', 4' × 12', or 4' × 16'. Professionals normally use 4' × 12' sheets to cut down on the time used hanging and making seams. Four-by-eight sheets are much easier to handle and are the common choice of most homeowners.

Typical drywall construction consists of a finished side, normally white- or cream-colored, a gypsum center, and a paper backing. The edges of drywall may be straight, tapered, squared, bevelled, rounded, or tongue-and-groove.

Hanging Drywall

When drywall is being hung, it can be attached to studs and joists with nails, screws, or staples. Most professionals use drywall screws and electric screw guns to install the wallboard. One advantage of screws is that they are less likely to work loose than are nails. If a nail works its way loose, it will dimple or pop the drywall finish.

When drywall is being attached to joists and studs, nails should be driven extra deep to create a dimple in the drywall (Illus. 14-1). Screws should be driven tight to make a depression in the wallboard. These depressions can be filled with joint compound to hide the nail (or screw) heads. When nailing, use a crown-head hammer. This type of hammer has a rounded-out head that makes good dimples.

Gypsum board is heavy and brittle. It's best to carry gypsum boards in a vertical position. If two people try to carry a board that's laid out in its full width, the weight of the board can cause it to break.

Drywall can be cut in many ways. You can use a keyhole or drywall saw to cut it (Illus. 14-2). A jigsaw or a sabre saw will also do a fine job of cutting gypsum. A utility knife is the tool used by most professionals to cut drywall (Illus. 14-3). Score the drywall with the utility knife and then break it at the scored seam. Many people use

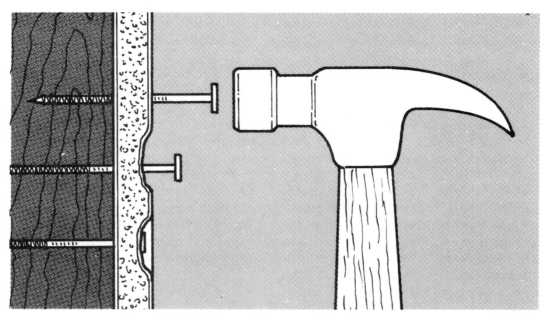

Illus. 14-1. Driving nail into wallboard to create a dimple. Drawing courtesy of Georgia-Pacific Corp.

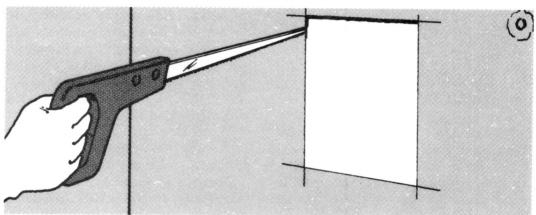

Illus. 14-2. Drywall saw. Drawing courtesy of Georgia-Pacific Corp.

Illus. 14-3. Cutting drywall with a utility knife. Drawing courtesy of Georgia-Pacific Corp.

Illus. 14-4. Drywall brace. Drawing courtesy of Georgia-Pacific Corp.

T-squares, 2 × 4s, or chalk lines to provide a guide for a straight cut.

Hanging Ceilings

When both the walls and ceilings will be covered with drywall, start by hanging the ceilings. Once you've hung the ceilings the drywall installed on the stud walls will help to support them.

The ceiling drywall is attached to the exposed ceiling joists. Cutouts will have to be made for any ceiling-mounted electrical boxes or fixtures. The hard part is getting the drywall up on the ceiling. Due to its weight, drywall isn't easy to install above your head. However, there's a way to ease the task.

A couple of strips of scrap 2 × 4 material will make a brace to hold the drywall in place (Illus. 14-4). This type of brace is known either as a T-brace, or a "dead man." To make the brace, nail a length of 2 × 4, about 3′ long, onto the end of a 2 × 4 that's long enough to reach the ceiling with a little left over.

Once this brace is made, it can be wedged under the drywall to hold it to the ceiling. The T-arm will rest under the drywall and the long section of the brace will be wedged between the subfloor and the ceiling. If two people raise the drywall to the ceiling, this brace allows the second person to release

the drywall once the T-arm is wedged into place.

By using two tall ladders and two T-braces, it's possible to hang a ceiling by yourself. It's not easy, but it's possible. Rest the drywall atop the ladders. Leave a couple of feet of the wallboard hanging over each end of the ladders. Put the first T-brace under one end and raise the drywall with the brace. Wedge the brace against the floor and raise the other end of the drywall with the other brace.

Hanging Walls

Hanging walls can be done by applying the drywall either vertically or horizontally. Color plate W shows a photo of this process. Choose the method that will result in the least waste and the fewest seams. If you hang walls vertically, you won't need any help. Hanging the walls horizontally will generally result in fewer joints, but it's more difficult to do without a helper. There are, however, some tricks that will make horizontal hanging easier without help.

Nail large nails to the studs to provide temporary support for the drywall panel, or nail a 2 × 4 ledger horizontally across the wall. The drywall can rest on the ledger while you attach the drywall to the studs. With either method you'll have to make cutouts for electrical boxes, water supplies,

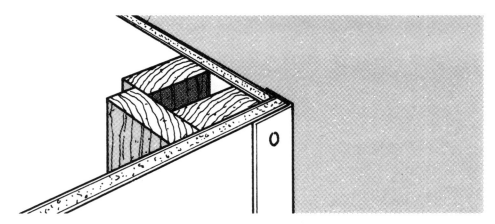

Illus. 14-5. Metal corner bead. Photo courtesy of Georgia-Pacific Corp.

drain arms, and other things that shouldn't be covered up.

Corner Bead

Metal corner bead is installed on the outside edges of most corners and exposed edges of drywall (Illus. 14-5). These metal strips provide protection to exposed corners and edges. The strips are perforated and can be nailed or screwed to wall studs. The corner

bead is designed to retain joint compound for a smooth finish.

Applying Tape & Joint Compound

Applying tape and joint compound (Illus. 14-6) requires practice and patience.

Some joint compound (or "mud," as it's called in the trade), needs to be mixed with water, but other types are ready to use right

Illus. 14-6. Materials needed to finish drywall. Drawing courtesy of Georgia-Pacific Corp.

out of the bucket. Refer to the manufacturer's instructions. You'll use a wide (4") putty knife to spread the "mud."

The tape used in finishing drywall isn't sticky. It's a wide band of paper that comes on a roll (Illus. 14-7). The tape can be torn or cut, and it's flexible.

Applying the First Coat
When applying the first coat of joint compound, spread it over seams, corner bead, and dimples (Illustrations 14-8, 14-9, 14-10, and 14-11). Don't spread too much at one time; it's best to coat one seam at a time. The first coat of mud should be about 3" wide, and it should be applied generously.

Once the mud is in place, lay a strip of tape on it and over the seam. Use the putty knife to work the tape down into the mud. The tape should sink deep into it. Next, smooth out the mud and feather it away at the edges of the tape. Continue this process on all the seams.

When filling in nail dimples, tape isn't necessary (Illus. 14-12). Simply apply joint compound in the depressions until it is flush with the drywall. Smooth the compound out with your putty knife and let it dry.

You don't need tape when applying mud to corner beads. The metal strips are meant to take on the mud directly. However, at in-

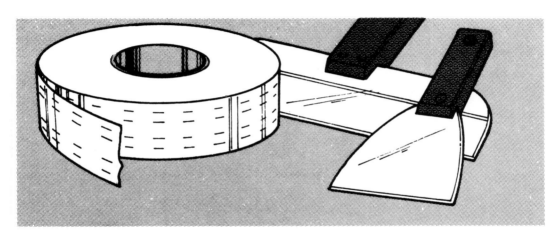

Illus. 14-7. Drywall tape. Drawing courtesy of Georgia-Pacific Corp.

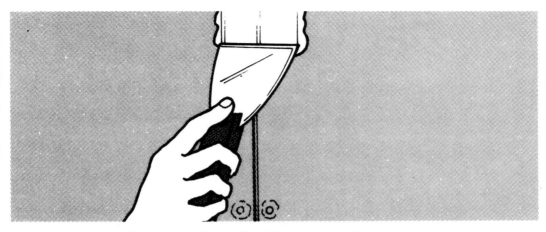

Illus. 14-8. Spreading joint compound on a seam. Drawing courtesy of Georgia-Pacific Corp.

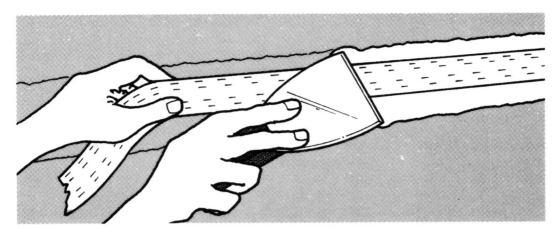

Illus. 14-9. Applying drywall tape. Drawing courtesy of Georgia-Pacific Corp.

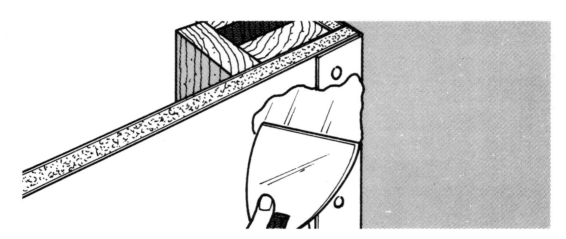

Illus. 14-10. Spreading mud on an outside corner. Drawing courtesy of Georgia-Pacific Corp.

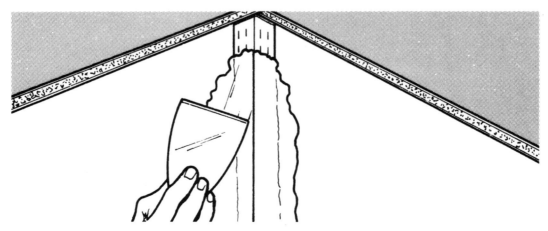

Illus. 14-11. Spreading mud on an inside corner. Drawing courtesy of Georgia-Pacific Corp.

side corners, where there's no bead, tape is required.

To prepare for the tape, run a line of mud down the inside corner. Cut the length of tape you'll need and fold it to fit into the corner. Work the tape into the mud as you did with the other seams.

Now wait for the compound to dry. Under average conditions, it should dry overnight. In damp or cold conditions, the drying may take longer. Under such conditions, use some heat to speed it up. The heat should be distributed evenly, and it shouldn't be too great. Direct or excessive heat can cause the joint compound to crack, and it will become hard to work with.

Applying the Second Coat

After the first coat of joint compound is dry, you'll be ready to apply the second. The second coat is applied atop the first coat, but it should be much wider than the first, which had a width of about 3″. The second coat should be about 6″ wide. Go over all of the original mud with a second coat (Illus. 14-13). This coat will also have to dry before you can move on.

The Third Coat

The third coat is usually the final finish. Before applying this last coat, you have some sanding to do. Sand the second coat of compound, first with medium-grit sandpaper,

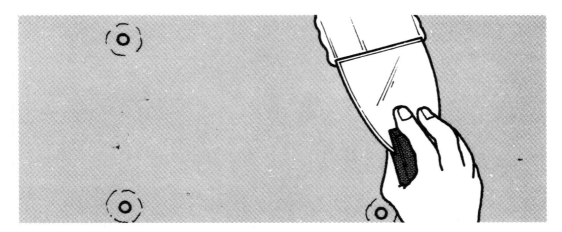

Illus. 14-12. Filling in nail dimples. Drawing courtesy of Georgia-Pacific Corp.

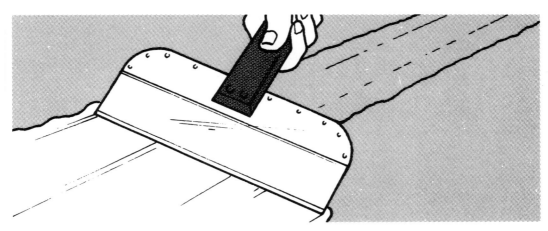

Illus. 14-13. Second coat of drywall mud. Drawing courtesy of Georgia-Pacific Corp.

and then with fine-grit. You could use pieces of sandpaper, a sanding block, or a sanding block that attaches to a long handle. Use soft strokes to avoid scarring the wallboard. A good dust mask is very helpful.

When you're ready to put on the third coat of mud, spread it about 10″ wide. As you spread the mud, feather the edges. The wider strip and feathered edges will make it easier to hide the seams. Cover the nail dimples with broad strokes and feather the edges. The final coat of mud is applied much more lightly than the previous coats were.

Sanding

After the final coat of mud has dried, you'll be ready for the finish sanding. Since the third coat of mud was applied in a very thin layer, it will be easier to sand than the second coat was. Use a fine-grit sandpaper for the finish sanding. When this step is complete, you'll be ready to clean up and to prime and paint the walls. Chapter 15 discusses doors, cabinets, and interior trim. You may want to tend to these items before painting. Chapter 16 will instruct you in the best ways to handle priming, painting, and staining.

15
Interior Doors, Cabinets & Trim

Once you're ready to install interior doors, cabinets, and trim, your job is almost done. Now you're about to begin what can be a tedious task.

When your job is finished, the insulation won't be seen. At the end of the job, you won't notice the routing of the electrical wires, nor the plumbing. But, you *will* see doors, cabinets, and trim, and you'll see them daily. Since the finish work is what *will* be seen, you'll want this part of your work to be attractive. Rough work doesn't have to look good, it only has to be functional. Trim work must look good, or the entire job will suffer.

Trim work can be deceptive. A novice might watch a trim carpenter and assume that he could do the same job. In reality, trim work can be demanding and frustrating. This phase of the job can also be expensive, because finish-trim materials are expensive. Unlike missing a cut on a 2 × 4, a mistake made when cutting a handrail can be *very* expensive. Screwing cabinets to a

wall may *look* simple, but it can require extensive skill.

Interior Doors

When it comes to choosing interior doors, you'll have many options. The cost of these doors fluctuates greatly. Will you use flat luan doors or six-panel doors? If you decide on six-panel doors, will they be real wood or a composite material? Do you know the difference between a left-hand and a right-hand door (Illus. 15-1)? Should you buy standard slab doors or prehung units? What hardware should be used on the doors? Questions about interior doors are many. In this section, these questions will be answered. Also, installation methods will be discussed.

Standard Doors

Standard doors are often called "slab"

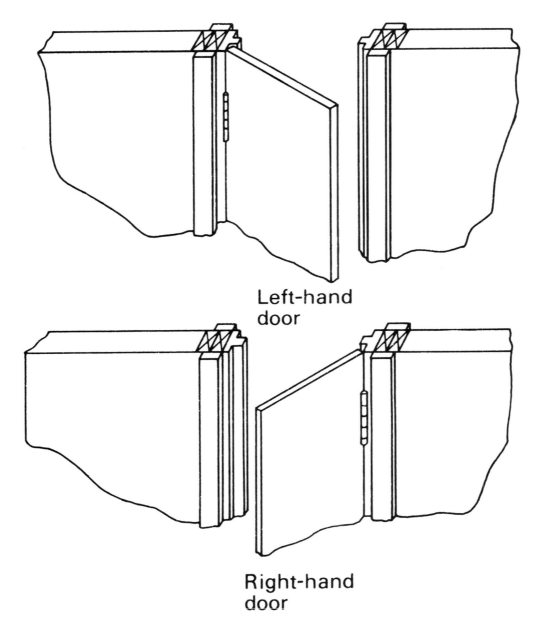

Illus. 15-1. Direction of swing for right- and left-hand doors. Drawing courtesy of U.S. Dept. of Agriculture

doors. These doors are sold individually; they don't come with trim packages, nor are they prehung. The installation of a slab door is best left to professionals, since installing such a door can be a complicated project. Beginners would be much better off purchasing prehung doors. However, since some will still want to install standard doors, here's how it's done.

Building the Jamb

Before standard doors can be hung, a doorjamb must be built (Illus. 15-2). A doorjamb consists of a head jamb and two side jambs. Jamb material is normally a one-by material. The width of the jamb will be determined by the wall covering on the stud wall. If a standard ½″ drywall is used, the jamb will typically have a width of 4⁹⁄₁₆″.

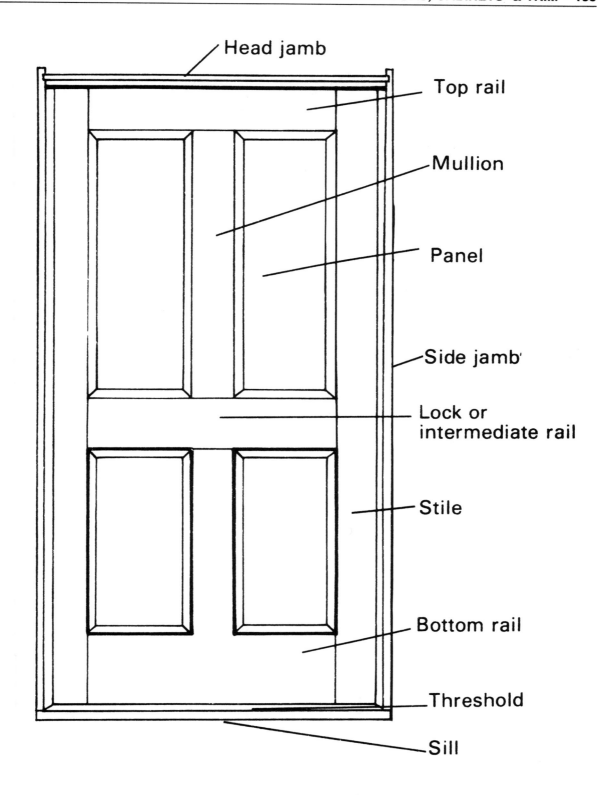

Illus. 15-2. Door components detail. Drawing courtesy of U.S. Dept. of Agriculture

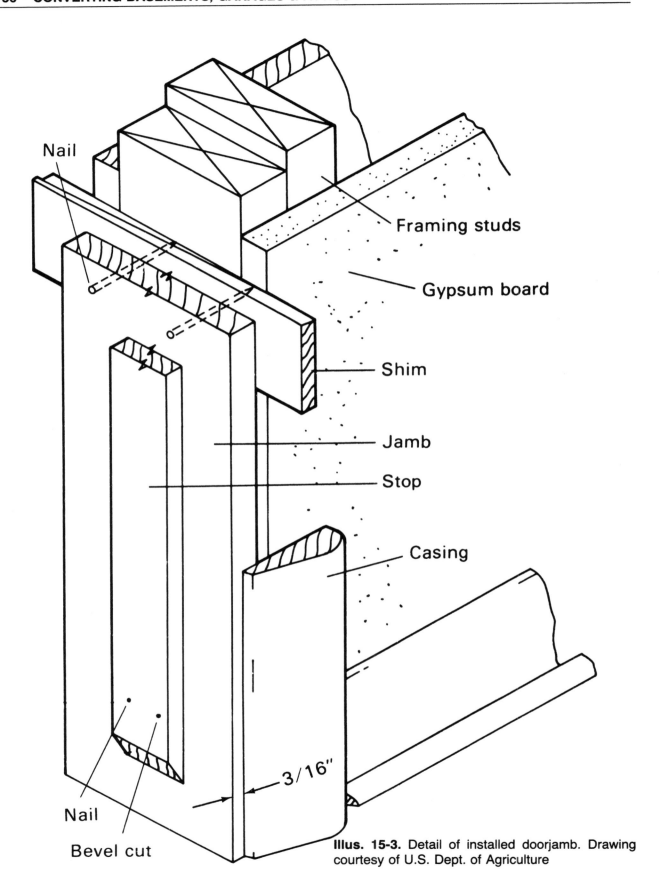

Nail

Framing studs

Gypsum board

Shim

Jamb

Stop

Casing

Nail

Bevel cut

3/16"

Illus. 15-3. Detail of installed doorjamb. Drawing courtesy of U.S. Dept. of Agriculture

When building a doorjamb, consider the size of the door and the height of the floor covering. Most standard doors are 6'8" high. Door widths vary. On average, the jamb opening should be about 2½" wider than the door. Three inches is a standard figure for the gap above the door and between the side jambs. Remember to allow for the floor covering. A floor covered with vinyl flooring will require the door to be hung lower than will a floor covered with a pad and a carpet.

Once the jamb is assembled, it should be set into place and levelled (Illus. 15-3). It may be necessary to cut one of the side jambs to a shorter length to make the jamb level. The next step is to find the proper location for the hinges.

Installing Hinges

Door hinges are usually set with the bottom edge of the lower hinge about 11" above the bottom of the door. The upper hinge is usually mounted with its top edge about 7" below the top of the door. If a third hinge is used, it's usually centered between the two other hinges.

Lay the first hinge on the edge of the door. Allow the barrel of the hinge to protrude past the edge of the door by about ⅛". Trace around the hinge with a pencil or utility knife to mark the hinge location on the door. Next, place the door in the jamb. This is only a temporary setting to allow you to mark the hinge locations on the jamb. Once the door is in the jamb, allow a small clearance between the top of the door and the head jamb, say about ¹⁄₁₆". Mark the jamb to indicate hinge locations.

Now you'll be ready to chisel recesses for the hinges in the door and in the side jamb. Use a sharp wood chisel. Start by cutting with the chisel running parallel to the door. Once cuts are made, chisel them out with the chisel perpendicular to the door. The recesses should be deep enough to allow the hinges to mount flush into them.

Shimming the Hinge Jamb

It is necessary to shim the doorjamb to make it firm and level. The shim material can be scrap wood, but most carpenters use cedar shingles. Start by shimming the side jamb where the hinges will be mounted. Place shims between the side jamb and the rough framing. Check the side jamb to see that it's level in both directions, and nail through the side jamb and shims into the rough framing. Finish nails should be used for this application, normally 8d nails.

Hanging the Door

Before shimming the remainder of the jamb, you should hang the door. Start by removing the hinge pins from the hinges. Keep the hinge halves together so that they can be matched during the installation. Install the hinge plates on the door, first. Be sure the mounting screws recess into the hinge plate. Next, install the hinge plates on the side jamb, matching hinge-halves with the ones mounted on the door.

Hanging the door will be easy if you have someone to help, but it can be done alone. Lift the door into place and allow the hinge-halves to go together. When the top hinge-halves are in proper alignment, insert a hinge pin, but don't drive it in tight. The pin should hold the hinge-halves together, but it shouldn't be permanently set at this time. Continue this process, working from the top to the bottom.

Shimming the Rest of the Jamb

With the door in place, you'll be ready to shim the rest of the jamb. Place shims between the jamb and the rough framing. When the jamb is level in all directions, try swinging the door through the jamb. Then, place the door in the closed position. When the door is closed, there should be approximately ¹⁄₁₆" of open space between the edges of the door and the jamb. When the door is properly positioned, nail through the jamb and shims into the framing.

Installing Hardware

When installing hardware, you may have to drill into the door. Some doors come predrilled for hardware, but others don't. Before drilling into the door, check the instructions that came with it. Most door-knobs require a hole just over 2″ in diameter, but hardware requirements vary, so follow the instructions that come packed with the hardware. Most instructions will include a template as a guide for cutting and drilling the door. Once you've installed the latch, strike plate, and doorknob, you'll be ready to put on the doorstop.

Installing Doorstop Trim

Installing doorstop trim is easy. Doorstop is sold in stock sizes; just ask for doorstop material. Close the door and make sure that the latch is working. With the door closed, nail the doorstop into place. The doorstop will run vertically on each side jamb and horizontally along the head jamb. The stop should be nailed in place so that it's firm against the door, but don't apply undue pressure. Use finish nails for this phase of the job, normally 4d nails.

Installing Door Casing

The last major step is to install the door casing. Six-penny finish nails are frequently used for this part of the job. Cut the trim to fit around the doorjamb. Hold the casing off the edge of the jamb by about ⅛″ to allow clearance for working with hinge pins. Once the trim is tacked into place and it fits satisfactorily, drive the nails in tight. Use a nail punch to recess the nails into the trim. All that's left is to drive down the hinge pins, and you'll be done.

Prehung Doors

Prehung doors will save time and frustration. When you buy prehung doors, they come as a unit, ready to set into the rough opening. The doorjamb is built, the door is hung and drilled for hardware, and even the trim casing is included and preassembled. Buy prehung doors, unless you just can't get the door you love in a prehung unit.

Cabinets

Hanging and setting cabinets can be tricky. When the floor or the walls aren't level, creative adjustments must be made. While setting a base cabinet in place or screwing wall cabinets to the studs may look easy, it isn't always so.

Base Cabinets

Base cabinets are cabinets that rest on the floor. When the floor and the walls are level, base cabinets are easy to install. Standard base cabinets are generally about 32½″ high. Once a countertop is installed on a base cabinet, the finished height is usually around 36″.

Cabinet material might consist of solid wood, plywood, or particleboard. Many ready-made ("production" or "stock") cabinets use a mixture of these materials. Although stock cabinets are much more economical than custom cabinets, the cost of stock cabinets can exceed your budget. Cabinets constitute one of the largest single expenses in a remodelling job.

With base cabinets, there are many options. Do you want dovetail joints or butt joints? Dovetail joints will hold up better than butt joints will. Base cabinets may have doors, drawers, appliance openings, or special accessories. Many base cabinets have a combination of drawers and doors. An important consideration in choosing a drawer base is to see how well the drawers glide. If the drawers will see frequent use (and they usually do), insist on a cabinet with quality glides and rollers.

Before buying or installing cabinets, design the layout. Most stores that sell cabinets will be happy to come to your home to measure the job. Then, the supplier will often provide a sketch or computer-generated drawing to show you what the proposed cabinets will look like (Illus. 15-4). Make your design decisions and changes before buying the cabinets. Also take into consideration your need for filler strips and accessory pieces.

Illus. 15-4. Kitchen cabinets with panel doors. Drawing courtesy of Quaker Maid, A Division of WCI, Inc.

Wall Cabinets

The height of standard wall cabinets will vary, but most are available with widths as narrow as 9″. Most wall cabinets are available in a range of widths, usually in 3″ increments. Do you want cabinet doors made with hardware pulls or finger grooves? When shopping for wall cabinets, look for quality in the shelves and latches. Shelf holders should be adjustable, to allow for various shelf heights. Magnetic latches are less likely to break and should last much longer than plastic latches.

Installing Cabinets

Before installing cabinets, check a few things. If cabinets aren't installed level, drawers and doors may not operate properly, and cabinets will be crooked. New construction presents fewer levelling problems than do old walls and floors. However, even in new construction, walls and floors aren't always level. Before you install the cabinets, check the floors and walls. If these areas are out of plumb, you'll need to shim the cabinets.

Wall Cabinets

Most people install wall cabinets first to avoid damaging the base cabinets. The first consideration is how high to hang the cabinets. This measurement varies, but as a general rule, hang them so that the top of the cabinet is about 84" above the floor. Once you determine the desired height, mark a level line as a reference point. Next, find the wall studs. If necessary, you can do this by probing the wall where the cabinet will hang. The back of the cabinet will conceal any holes made by probing. Make a measurement from one corner to the stud for reference. Most wall studs will be installed 16" on center.

Start with a corner cabinet. Hanging wall cabinets is much easier if you have some help. Getting cabinets into position and keeping them there is difficult for one person. Even with help, you'll probably want to use some 2 × 4 prop sticks to hold the wall cabinets up.

Once the cabinet is in place and level, drill holes through the back of the cabinet and into the wall studs. The holes should be near the top of the cabinet. There's frequently a mounting strip in the cabinet for the screws to penetrate. Install screws to hold the cabinet in place. At this time, the screws don't need to be tight. In most cases, there will be some shimming and final adjustments to be made before the screws are driven for good.

After the first cabinet is installed, install the adjacent cabinet in the same manner. When you have two wall cabinets in place, attach them. The first step in joining the two cabinets is to get them into proper alignment. Adjust them until they are in the proper horizontal and vertical position. You can use C-clamps to hold them together and in place. Double-check the alignment. Then, use ¼" screws to attach the two cabinets to each other. Some people prefer nuts and bolts for the joining process. The screws or bolts should be placed near the top and bottom of the cabinet sidewalls.

Rather than hanging the cabinets one by one, you could join them on the floor and raise the entire row at one time. If you have enough help to lift the completed row, this method can be fast and easy.

Once the row of cabinets is complete and in position, you can screw the units tightly to the wall. Frequently check to be sure the cabinets remain level. Once the row is in-stalled, add filler strips as needed. The filler strips will be of the same finish as the cabinets, and they'll conceal any gaps where the cabinets meet walls or other objects.

Depending upon your design, you could install either a soffit or a valance. These are trim boards, in the same finish as the cabinets, to close up the space between the top of the cabinets and the ceiling. To install these trims, you must first attach a nailing surface to the ceiling to provide a place for the trim to be attached.

Base Cabinets

Base cabinets are easier than wall cabinets to install. Start with a corner cabinet and build the row *out*. It may be necessary to shim under the cabinets to keep them level. Base cabinets should be attached to each other in the same way as are wall cabinets. Check to see that the base cabinets are level, both vertically and horizontally.

If you're working with a base cabinet that doesn't have a back, you'll need to install cleats. Cleats are just strips of wood that support the countertop. The cleats (or "ledgers," as they're sometimes called) are attached to wall studs. The ledgers should be installed level and at the same height as the front of the cabinet.

Countertops

Countertops are next. There are numerous choices in countertop styles and materials. Your supplier should be able to show you many samples. The easiest way to deal with countertops is to have them measured, delivered, and installed by professionals. If you give your dealer the brand and model of your sink, he can cut the sink hole for you. Then, when the countertop is delivered, just install the sink. Wait until the cabinets are installed to order the top. Since jobs don't always work out as they're drawn on paper, ordering the top before the cabinets are installed could result in a top that wouldn't fit.

When you look down on the base cabinets,

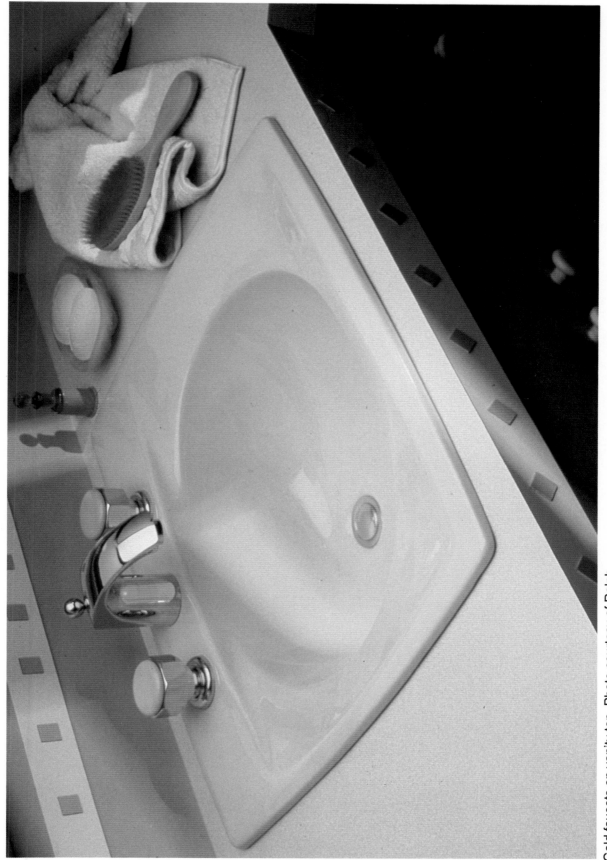

Gold faucets on vanity top. Photo courtesy of Ralph Wilson Plastics Co.

Sitting room. Photo by Mannington Resilient Floors

Attic bathroom with a spa. Photo by Mannington Resilient Floors

Office with roof window. Photo courtesy of Velux-America, Inc.

Illus. 15-5. Pantry cabinet. Photo courtesy of Wood-Mode, Inc.

Illus. 15-6. A kitchen badly in need of renovation

Illus. 15-7. The new cabinets are all in place

Illus. 15-8. Notice the recessed lighting

Illus. 15-9. The completed kitchen

Illus. 15-10. Detail of the new countertop

you should see some triangular blocks of wood in the corners. These triangles provide a place to attach the counter to the cabinet. Before setting the counter in place, drill holes through these mounting blocks. Confine the holes to a location that will allow you to install screws from inside the cabinet. It may be a good idea to drill the holes on an angle, towards the middle of the cabinet, to allow more freedom when installing screws.

Set the countertop in place and check its fit. When the top is in position, install screws from below, through the holes in the triangular blocks. Make sure the screws are long enough to penetrate the counter but not long enough to penetrate and ruin the top.

If you must cut your own sink hole, use the template that came with your sink (if you have a new sink). If you're using an old sink, turn it upside down and set it on the counter, in the proper location. Lightly trace around the sink rim with a pencil. Remove

the sink and draw a new outline inside the original tracing. When you guess how large the hole should be, it's better to cut it too small than too large. You must make the hole smaller than the lines you traced around the sink. There must be enough counter left to support the sink rim.

To cut the sink hole, drill a hole in the countertop. Using a reciprocating saw, place the blade in the hole you drilled. Cut slowly along the interior line. Don't get your lines confused; cutting to the outside line will mean a ruined countertop. When the hole's finished, try putting the sink in it. If necessary, expand the opening until the sink fits.

If you have limited space, there are many types of specialty cabinet available. Pantry cabinets can provide a lot of storage in a little space (Illus. 15-5). Illustrations 15-6 through 15-10 show new-cabinet installation. Some cabinets are equipped with built-in units, like tables and pull-down bins (Illus. 15-11). When installing cabinets in

Illus. 15-11. Slide-out table and pull-down bins. Photo courtesy of Wood-Mode, Inc.

Illus. 15-12. Over-toilet cabinet. Drawing courtesy of Quaker Maid, A Division of WCI, Inc.

Illus. 15-13. Pull-down cabinet. Drawing courtesy of Quaker Maid, A Division of WCI, Inc.

small bathrooms, good cabinet selection can provide additional storage (Illustrations 15-12, 15-13, and 15-14).

Interior Trim

Interior trim is easy to install, if you're good at cutting angles. First, find and mark stud locations. You will use 6d finish nails with most trim applications. A backsaw (Illus. 15-15) and mitre box (Illus. 15-16) are both inexpensive means to cut angles on trim material. Most professionals use power mitre saws, but a mitre box and backsaw will work fine.

The two most common baseboards are clam and colonial. Colonial baseboard is considered to be standard in fine construction. Baseboard is installed along walls to conceal gaps between the wallboard and floor (Illus. 15-17). When carpeting the floor, some people install the baseboard low and allow the carpet to conceal part of it. Others raise up the baseboard to allow for the thickness of the carpet and pad.

Cutting corners isn't difficult with a mitre box (Illus. 15-18). However, getting used to fitting the angles together can take some time. If you have a long run of baseboard, you may have to make a joint in the run. Instead of butting the two pieces of trim together, you should cut angles that will allow the two trim pieces to lie over each other (Illus. 15-19). This is often called a lap joint. By cutting a lap joint, you'll have an even flow in the trim. When baseboard meets door casing, it simply butts against the casing. If baseboard heating units will be attached to the walls, omit baseboard trim in the area to be occupied by the heating unit.

If the finished floor covering will be a thin

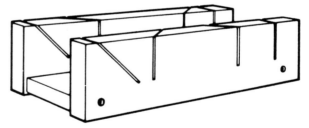

Illus. 15-14. Linen cabinet. Drawing courtesy of Quaker Maid, A Division of WCI, Inc.

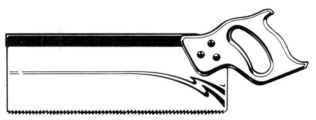

Illus. 15-15. Backsaw. Drawing courtesy of Georgia-Pacific Corp.

Illus. 15-16. Mitre box. Drawing courtesy of Georgia-Pacific Corp.

vinyl material, shoe mould should be used. Install the baseboard trim first. Then, install the finish floor. After the floor is in place, add the shoe mould, which is a small trim piece that covers the joints where the flooring meets the baseboard.

Chair rail and crown moulding are installed with the same basic techniques. Chair rail goes on the wall, at a sufficient height to prevent the backs of chairs from damaging the wall. Crown moulding is installed where the wall meets the ceiling (Il-

lus. 15-20). Once you're comfortable cutting angles, you'll be able to work with any of the other trim materials.

Final Comments

Take your time when you do finish work. You must be willing to be patient and precise if you want a good-looking job. Trim work isn't hard physically, but it's *mentally* demanding.

Illus. 15-17. Baseboard and shoe-mould installation. Drawing courtesy of Georgia-Pacific Corp.

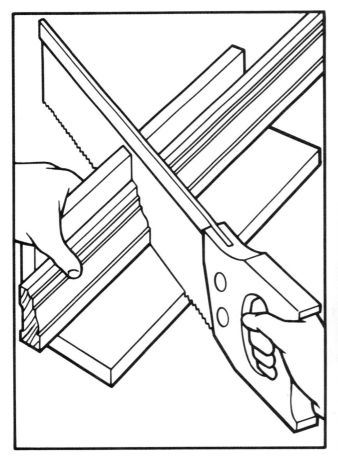

Illus. 15-18. Backsaw in mitre box. Drawing courtesy of Georgia-Pacific Corp.

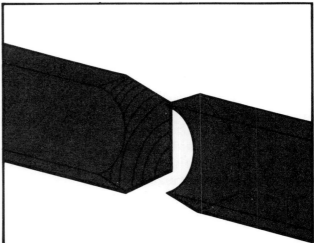

Illus. 15-19. Trim splicing detail. Drawing courtesy of Georgia-Pacific Corp.

Illus. 15-20. Crown moulding. Photo courtesy of Lis King and Focal Point

16
Paint & Stain

Anyone can do paint and stain work, but it takes special knowledge to do it *right*. The public generally perceives painting as a job that doesn't require in-depth knowledge or skill, but this is a false perception. Just because painters aren't subject to the same professional licensing requirements as plumbers and electricians doesn't mean that painters don't have to know what they're doing.

Painting is one phase of a job that most homeowners can do and achieve satisfactory results. *How* you paint can have much to do with how long the job holds up and how good the job looks. This chapter will show you the easy way to paint or stain your project, and it will alert you to some pitfalls.

Exterior Painting

Exterior painting includes painting the siding, windows, exterior trim, foundations, or railings. If you'll be building a dormer, you'll have some high-elevation exterior painting to do. This work, primarily due to its location, can be dangerous. Before painting your dormer, observe good judgment and safety procedures.

Some dormers can be painted while you're standing on the surrounding roof, but most such jobs will require the use of ladders or scaffolding. With whichever method you use to reach the area to be painted, make sure that the climbing device is secure and safe. Cordon off the area around your ladder to avoid having someone run into it, possibly knocking you off. Be extremely careful when handling ladders around electrical wires.

Types of Paints & Primers

The two types of paint to consider are latex and oil-based paint. Most painters believe that if a house is to be painted white, it should have an oil-based primer and paint. It's generally thought best to use an oil-based primer and a latex paint if the house will be painted a color other than white.

Primer is normally white. If you're painting your house white, don't have the primer tinted. However, if you are painting with a color other than white, ask your paint dealer to tint the primer to match the finish color. Avoid tinting the primer so that it becomes either much darker or much lighter than the finish paint.

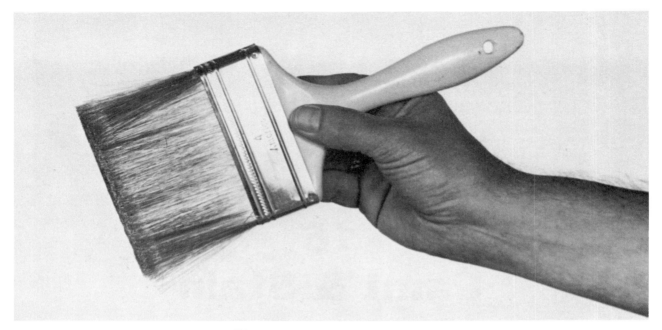

Illus. 16-1. Four-inch paintbrush

Illus. 16-2. Brush for painting trim (2″)

Should you use flat paint or gloss paint? Flat paint is normally used for siding, and gloss paint is used for trim and windows. Gloss paint is easier to clean than flat, but gloss shows more irregularities in the painted surface than flat does.

Preparing to Paint

Use dropcloths to protect the surrounding roof, existing home, and lawn and shrubbery. Paper dropcloths are easy to use and inexpensive, and they're a good choice for the occasional painter. Plastic dropcloths

Illus. 16-3. Midsize (3″) paintbrush

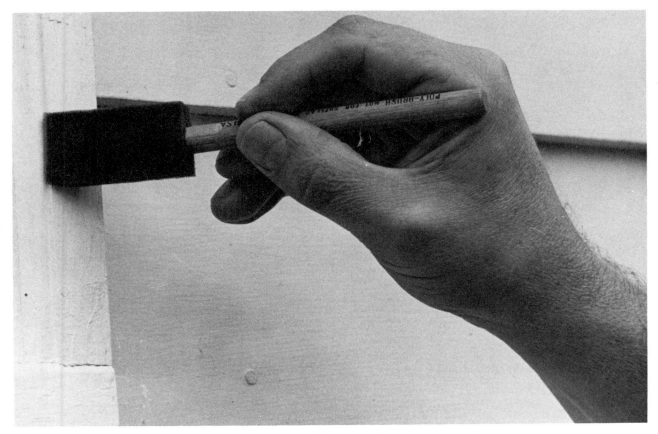

Illus. 16-4. Foam applicator

are slippery and do not contain paint well. Light canvas dropcloths are the professional's choice, but they're expensive, and most homeowners will never need them again.

Your paint dealer will shake the paint for you, but mix it again before using it. Too many people try to use the little wooden stirrers to mix paint in a gallon can. This procedure won't get you a good mix. Pour the contents of the gallon cans into a larger container, like a five-gallon bucket. The larger container will allow you to mix the paint thoroughly.

Methods of Application

The usual ways to paint are brushing, rolling, and spraying. For dormer additions, a 4″ brush is probably the best choice (Illus. 16-1). You should also have a 1½″ (Illus. 16-2) or 2″ brush for painting windows and small trim. A 3″ brush (Illus. 16-3) is good for window frames and some trim. Foam applicators are also good for painting trim (Illus. 16-4). Nylon brushes are usually used with latex paint, and bristle brushes are used with oil-based paints. Rollers don't work well with most types of siding, and sprayers can get messy, especially if the wind is blowing.

Start painting at the top of the exterior wall and work your way down. If you'll be painting the window grids or the trim a different color or with a different paint, paint the windows first. If you don't paint the windows first, when you come back to paint them you may damage the paint on the siding. Apply enough primer paint to cover the surface, but don't brush it on too heavy. What you want is a good coat of primer, followed by an even coat of finish paint. Don't paint a surface that's bathed in direct sunlight. Check with the manufacturer's suggestions, but most paint should not be applied in temperatures below 50 °F, or if the weather's extremely hot.

If you must thin your paint, do it a little at a time and in a container other than the mix bucket. Most painters use a small pail to hold the paint they're using at the moment. This pail is a good place to thin the paint. If you miscalculate the thinning, you've only wasted a small percentage of your paint, not the entire mix bucket.

Apply the paint *with* the grain of the wood, that is (normally), horizontally. If you use oil-based paint, the surface must be completely dry. If it has rained recently, postpone your painting until the sun has dried the siding.

If you use a sprayer, be advised that paint leaving a sprayer can wind up in other than the place intended. On windy days your paint may even blow over onto a neighbor's house.

Exterior Staining

Exterior staining is not the same as painting. Stain is available in latex or oil, but oil-based stain is the common choice among professionals. Latex stain does not penetrate the wood as well as does an oil stain. When choosing a type of stain, you will normally have three choices: solid, semisolid, and semitransparent.

Solid Stain

Solid stain looks like thin paint. Unlike most stains, solid stains can be applied over paint. This procedure is usually done only under special circumstances, but it is possible.

Semisolid Stain

Semisolid stains provide excellent penetration and protection of wood. While its name may imply a thick, paintlike substance, semisolid stain is thin and it doesn't provide a heavy visual cover.

Semitransparent Stain

Semitransparent stains are at their best on rough wood surfaces. These stains protect against moisture damage and are available in a wide range of colors.

Application Methods

Stains are usually best applied with a brush, although they can also be applied with a sprayer or with a roller. You can even apply stain with a rag, a sponge, or special staining mittens. If you choose to use a brush, buy one with natural bristles. Synthetic-bristle brushes don't work as well as natural-bristle brushes. Apply two coats of stain, and, unlike in painting, the second coat should be applied while the first coat is still wet. After the second coat dries for an hour or so, go over it with a sponge or rag to remove stain that didn't penetrate the wood. Latex stain doesn't penetrate wood. When using latex, apply two coats, but don't wipe off excess stain.

As you stain, stir the stain in the container frequently. If the stain isn't stirred regularly, the pigment in it will settle, causing different color shades. Use a lot of stain, the more the better. Unlike paint, stain should be applied liberally.

When you first choose a stain, try a little on a sample of the wood you'll be using it on. Because of the nature of stain, it will look different on various types of wood.

Painting Interior Walls & Ceilings

Painting new interior walls is certainly less stressful than painting a home's exterior, perched high upon an extension ladder. For painting interiors, a good stepladder should let you reach all the surfaces you need to paint.

Preparation
First, vacuum the room to remove all dust. If you don't vacuum, the paint will become textured with dust clumps. You should be working over a raw subfloor, so dropcloths won't be necessary.

Latex or Oil?
The decision between latex and oil paint is up to you. Most people use latex primer and latex paint. When buying your primer, have it tinted to match the finish color.

Applying Interior Paint
When applying interior paint, many contractors use only one coat of primer and one coat of paint. If the walls are in good shape this is all that should be needed, but some professionals prefer to apply two coats of primer for a better-looking job.

Usually the ceiling is painted first. Drywall finishers commonly texture ceilings. When this is done, paint is often mixed with joint compound. If you choose to do this, there will be no need for further ceiling painting. If you're doing a traditional paint job on the ceiling, use a roller. Sprayers are frequently used by professionals and are becoming increasingly popular with homeowners. When using a sprayer, it will take a little practice to set the spray correctly and to distribute the paint evenly.

When you paint ceilings with a roller, you will have to use a brush to cut in along the joint between the walls and the ceiling. Using a 2" or 3" brush, apply a strip of paint to the ceiling. The strip should be only a few feet long. As soon as you have this strip of wet paint, lay down the brush and pick up the roller. An extension handle on the roller will save you from making so many trips up and down a ladder. Use the roller to roll paint on the ceiling and over the wet strip. It is important to do your cut-ins a little at a time. If you try to cut in the whole ceiling before rolling on the paint, the cut-in section will dry. When you roll fresh paint over the dried cut-in paint, you'll get two different looks.

Continue this brush-roller combination until the ceiling is complete. Don't be stingy with the paint. When you roll paint out too thin, it will dry without covering the surface. When the ceiling is done, start on the walls. Again, you will have to cut in the joint between the wall and the ceiling, this time applying paint to the wall. Work in small sections and keep the brush-and-roller relay going, so that the paint doesn't dry.

After the first coat of paint, you may see imperfections that had been invisible until now. You may need to take time between the first and second coats to touch up the drywall. If you do touch-up work, be sure to vacuum any dust created before you return to painting.

Textured ceilings are very popular. If you texture the ceiling, there are many options available. Some contractors use drywall "mud" to create a ceiling texture, and others use special mixes, designed just for texturing (Illus. 16-5). You can use a variety of devices to apply texture, including a stiff paint brush (Illus. 16-6), a stipple paint-roller (Illus. 16-7), a stiff round brush (Illus. 16-8), and a trowel (Illus. 16-9).

Accent the interior painting with wall coverings and borders. Wall murals won't help you sell your home, but they can personalize a room (Illus. 16-10 and 16-11). A wide range of borders is available (Illus. 16-12). Borders may be used where walls meet ceilings or at the midpoint of the wall (Illus. 16-13).

Painting Interior Trim

Painting interior trim can be done before, during, or after painting the walls and ceilings. Many professionals recommend painting the trim in the same stages as you paint the walls. Normally, trim work is painted with gloss paint and walls are painted with flat paint. However, it isn't unusual to paint kitchens and bathrooms with a gloss paint, since gloss is easier to clean than flat. Since you'll be using two different types of paint and two different colors, you'll have to switch back and forth between walls and trim if you paint both at the same time.

Why go to the trouble of switching back and forth at the same phases? If you paint the walls to completion, you'll probably (accidentally) get some trim paint on the walls. By alternating between the trim and the walls in the same phase, you reduce the risk of creating extra work. Many people will still choose to paint the walls and then to paint the trim when the walls are finished. This will work if you're careful not to get trim paint on the walls.

Surprises
One surprise is the effect the primer coat

will have on some wood trim. Even if your trim is smooth when you apply the first coat of primer, the wood may become rough after the paint dries. This roughness can be annoying to anyone dusting and cleaning the trim. The roughness may be enough to snag cleaning rags and cause aggravation. After applying the first coat, check the texture of the trim. You may want to go over it with a light-grit sandpaper or steel wool to remove the rough spots. Vacuum the dust residue from the sanding before proceeding with your painting.

Filling the Holes
Filling the holes from the recessed finish nails will be required before final painting. Use wood putty and a small putty knife to fill and smooth out these holes.

Cutting In Windows & Trim
Cutting in windows and trim should be done as described in the earlier section on walls and ceilings. Work small areas and work with wet paint. When cutting in or edging, use a piece of cardboard to protect surfaces you don't want painted.

Staining Trim

Staining trim is often done before the trim is installed. If you plan to stain the trim, be sure to get clear wood, also known as stain-grade trim. This trim is a little more expensive than "finger-joint" trim, but it's the only type of trim to use when staining. Finger-joint trim can be painted without problems, but if you stain it, all the little finger joints will show through the stain. If you order prehung doors, specify stain-grade or clear trim. I have seen houses with stain-grade trim on the baseboards and finger-joint trim around the doors. This makes an odd and unappealing combination when the trim is stained.

A staining mitt or brush will make fast work of staining trim. If you use an oil-based stain and a brush, use a bristle brush. Trim

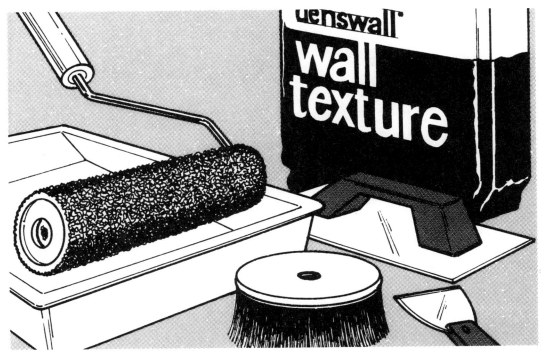

Illus. 16-5. Texturing materials. Drawing courtesy of Georgia-Pacific Corp.

Illus. 16-6. Stiff brush for texturing. Drawing courtesy of Georgia-Pacific Corp.

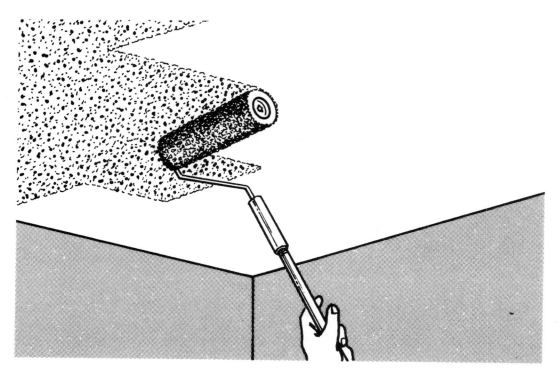

Illus. 16-7. Stipple roller for texturing. Drawing courtesy of Georgia-Pacific Corp.

Illus. 16-8. Stiff round brush for texturing. Drawing courtesy of Georgia-Pacific Corp.

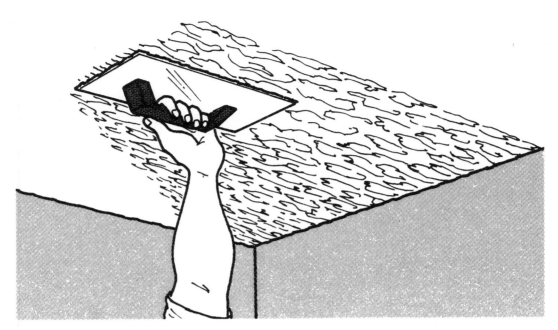

Illus. 16-9. Trowel for texturing. Drawing courtesy of Georgia-Pacific Corp.

should be stained before the walls are painted. It is common to stain trim before it's installed. Stain the trim and install it after it has dried. Go back and fill the nail holes with a colored putty (available in paint stores). Then, touch up the nail holes and cut marks with fresh stain. This is the fastest and easiest way to stain the trim.

Sealers

Some people don't use sealers on stained trim, but others do. If you want to seal the trim, use varnish or polyurethane. Sand the trim between each of two coats of sealer.

A paint dealer can provide more detailed information on the products you choose to use.

Illus. 16-10. Mural in a child's room. Photo courtesy of Lis King and Play Ball

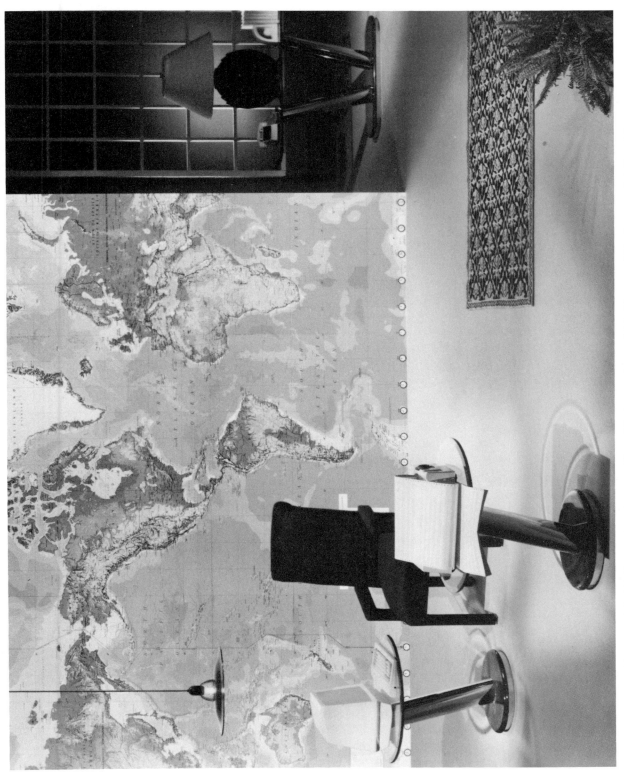

Illus. 16-11. Wall map in a home office. Photo courtesy of Lis King and Environmental Graphics

Illus. 16-12. Border materials. Photo courtesy of Lis King and MayFair

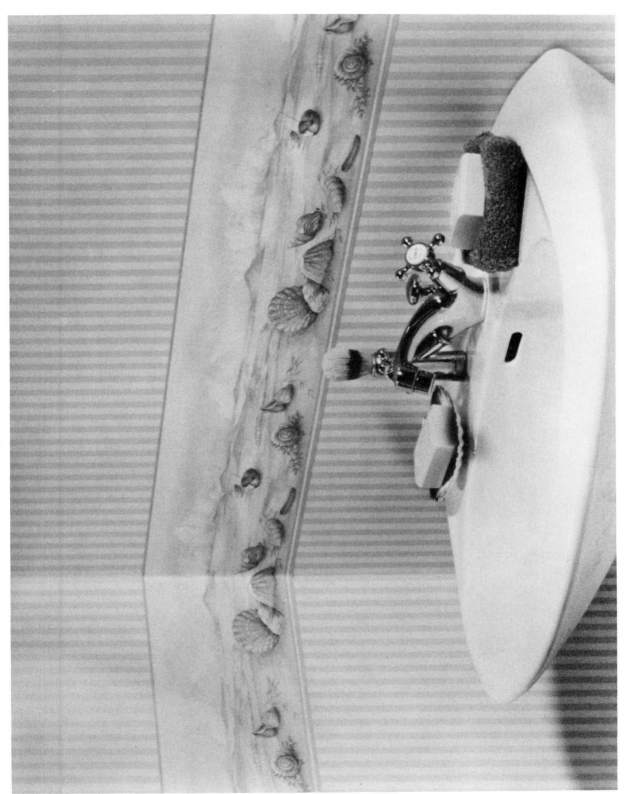

Illus. 16-13. Mid-wall border. Photo courtesy of Lis King and Forbo Wall Coverings, Inc.

17
Floor Coverings

Floor coverings come in many forms—carpet, vinyl sheet goods, ceramic tile, hardwood, softwood, and other options. Within each category are subcategories. The decisions required for choosing a finish floor covering and accessories can be complicated.

Installing finish floors requires special tools and skills. The tools can be rented or purchased, but the skills must be learned. With the cost of flooring, mistakes can be expensive. This is one part of your job where it might pay to call in professionals.

Carpet has become the standard floor covering for most rooms. Wall-to-wall carpeting dominates nearly every room in the home except the bathroom and the kitchen.

Types of Carpeting

There are numerous types and grades of carpeting. Much of the decision on what type of carpet to buy will depend on where you intend to install it.

Loop-Pile & Cut-Pile Carpet

Loop-pile and cut-pile carpet are the types found in most homes. They both consist of fibres that are stitched into a backing. If the fibres are uncut, the carpet is loop-pile. If the fibres are cut, the carpet is cut-pile. Carpet materials include acrylic, nylon, and polyester. Acrylic enjoys a long life. Nylon carpet is very strong and it resists stains. Polyester products are colorful and shiny.

Loop-pile carpet is usually installed over a pad and can be used in any room. The quality of the carpet pad plays an important role in the life of the carpet. If money is an issue, buy an excellent pad and a good carpet. The high-grade pad will be comfortable to walk on, and it will extend the life of the carpet.

Here's an experiment you can try at a carpet store. Take a carpet sample and lay it on the best quality pad. Stand on the carpet, and when you step off, see how long it takes for your footprints to disappear. Next, move the carpet sample to a low-grade pad and try the same test. You'll see that the same carpet on the better pad recovers its shape much more quickly than it does when it's on the cheaper pad.

Loop-pile carpet is normally laid over a pad and stretched to attach to tackless strips, which are either nailed or glued to the subfloor. When the carpet is stretched onto the strips, angled teeth on the strip grab and hold the carpet.

Foam-Back Carpet
Foam-back carpet is often considered a commercial carpet, but it's also a good choice for basement installations. Foam-back carpet is normally laid directly on the floor, without additional padding. The foam backing is glued or taped to the floor. If you're cost-conscious when finishing a basement, use foam-back carpet.

Carpet Squares
These easy-to-install squares of carpet have an adhesive backing and are simply pressed into place on the subfloor.

Planning a Carpet Installation

Planning a carpet installation requires some thought. Carpet has a pile, and the pile all leans in one direction. Carpet looks its best when you face the pile. For this reason, it is customary to install carpet with the pile pointing towards the entrance to a room.

Most carpet is made in widths that don't exceed 12'. If your room has dimensions greater than 12', you'll probably have to seam the carpet, but with enough searching you may be able to find a brand that offers widths wider than 12'. If you have to seam the carpet, keep the seam out of high-traffic spots.

Installing Loop-Pile & Cut-Pile Carpeting

Installing loop-pile and cut-pile carpeting can be tricky. First install the tackless strips (sometimes called "tack strips"), which are normally about 4' long and have sharp, angled teeth that bite into the carpet. Tackless strips come in different sizes; check with your carpet supplier for the proper size to use with your carpet and pad.

Tackless strips should be installed around the perimeter of the area to be carpeted. For doorways and cased openings, install metal trim strips. These strips are either folded over or nailed on top of the carpet to give a finished edge that people won't trip over.

Tackless strips should be installed maintaining a uniform distance from the wall. Check with your carpet supplier for the proper distance to maintain between the edge of the strip and the wall. The gap should be equal to two-thirds the thickness of the carpet.

Putting In the Pad
When putting in the pad, the tackless strips form a boundary. The pad should be installed to cover all the floor within the strips, but the pad shouldn't extend onto the strips. Check the manufacturer's recommendations to determine which side of the pad should lie on the floor.

Padding doesn't have to be installed in one piece; it can be installed in sections. When padding is installed on a wood subfloor, it's usually stapled to the floor. If you're installing the pad on a concrete floor, use an approved adhesive to hold it in place.

Cutting the Carpet
First, the carpet should be unrolled and flattened out, and it should be at room temperature. Cut the carpet so that there will be at least 3" of extra carpet in all directions. If you're working with a cut-pile carpet, cut it from the back. Make your measurements and use a chalk line or straightedge to make an even cut along the carpet backing. The cut can be made with a utility knife.

Loop-pile carpet should be cut from the finished side rather than from the backing. Make your measurement and use a straightedge for keeping the cut straight. The cutting can be done with a utility knife. There are also special carpet-cutting tools that can be used for this part of the job, such as a row-running knife.

Laying the Carpet
Laying the carpet will require the use of a

tool that stretches it. You might use a knee-kicker or a power stretcher. Either of these tools can be rented at most tool-rental outlets.

Put the carpet in place. The excess carpet should be turned up on all the walls. Use a utility knife to cut the carpet at the corners. Start the cut at the top of the upturned carpet and extend to a point close to the tack strip.

If your carpet must be seamed, the seam should be made before stretching the carpet. At the point of the seam, the two pieces of carpet should overlap each other by about 1″. Make sure that the pile of both pieces of carpet is running in the same direction. Using a row-running knife, cut a straight line along the edge of the overlapped carpet. The knife will run along the edge of the top piece of carpet, cutting the bottom piece of carpet.

When the cut is complete, remove the cut strip from beneath the top piece of carpet. Lay back the edges of both pieces of carpet

to expose the floor. Now lay a strip of hot-melt seaming tape on the floor. The tape should be laid so that the center of the tape is in line with the central point of where the two pieces of carpet will meet.

Run a hot iron over the seaming tape to activate it. Heat only small sections at a time, and maintain an iron temperature of about 250 °F. As the tape becomes sticky, roll the edges of the carpet pieces into place and butt them together. Continue this process, in small sections, until the complete seam is made.

Now you'll be ready to stretch the carpet. Ideally, you should have both a knee-kicker and a power stretcher. When you rent these tools, ask the supplier to show you how to use them properly. Start the stretching in a corner. Using the knee-kicker, attach the carpet to the tackless strips on two walls, at a corner.

Once the first corner is secured, use the power stretcher to secure the corner directly

Illus. 17-1. A newly completed room with freshly installed carpet

opposite the corner already done. Power stretchers have the ability to telescope out to long lengths, to be able to cover whole rooms. The knee-kicker will be used to secure the carpet between the previously secured locations. Two walls are done with the knee-kicker and two walls are done with the power stretcher.

When all of the carpet is attached to the tackless strips, cut away the excess carpet with a utility knife. Run the knife along the top of the installed carpet, cutting off the excess that's rolled up on the wall. Then, use a flat-bit screwdriver to tuck the remaining excess carpet into the gap between the tack strip and the wall.

At doorways and openings, cut the carpet to size and bend down the metal strip on top of the carpet. Use a wide block of wood and a hammer to drive the metal strip down tight. Place the block of wood on the strip and tap the block with the hammer. Don't hit the strip with just a hammer or the strip will be damaged. If you're using a nail-on strip of metal, put the metal in place and tack it down.

Installing carpet isn't simple. Seriously consider hiring a professional for this part of your job. Illus. 17-1 shows a newly installed carpet.

Installing Foam-Back Carpet

Installing foam-back carpet is very different from installing cut-pile or loop-pile carpet. There are no tackless strips needed, nor is it necessary to install separate padding. Foam-back carpet has a thin, built-in pad as a part of the carpet. You won't need stretchers, but you will need some adhesive or carpet tape.

Buy an adhesive that's recommended for the carpet you'll be installing; a carpet dealer can tell you which one to use. If you prefer to use tape to secure your carpet, the carpet dealer can recommend and supply two-sided tape.

Cut the foam-back carpet to a size to fit the area to be covered. Cut so that the carpet's a little larger than you think you will need. Lay the carpet in place and check the fit. Remove the carpet and trowel adhesive on the floor or install strips of carpet tape. A carpet dealer can tell you at what intervals and in what amounts to use the adhesive or the tape.

Place the carpeting over the tape or adhesive and work out any wrinkles in the carpet. You can use a length of 2 × 4 to push the wrinkles out. Lay the board on the carpet, with the wide side down, and push the board to the edge of the carpet, removing the wrinkles. When the carpet is flat, trim off the excess. If necessary, install shoe moulding to hide the joint between the carpet and the wall.

Vinyl Flooring

Sheet-vinyl flooring is a common choice for bathrooms and kitchens, and sometimes for basements. Sheet vinyl is generally more durable and easier to clean than individual vinyl tiles. Most vinyl sheet goods are available in widths of either 6' or 12'. Vinyl flooring, like carpet, can be a challenge to install. If you're willing to take your time and work precisely, you should be able to do the job yourself.

Surface conditions
The surface conditions of the area to be covered with vinyl are important. The surface should be flat and without cracks, bumps, or holes. Vinyl can be installed on wood or concrete, but if the surface isn't flat, imperfections will show up in the finished flooring.

Cracks in concrete floors, or even in wood floors, can be filled with special compounds designed expressly for that purpose (Illus. 17-2). Thin underlayment can be applied to even out the floor and cover bad spots. The goal is to have a surface that is flat, clean, dry, and free of oil, grease, or wax.

Prepare the Vinyl
Before installation, roll up the flooring with the finish side facing outward. Leave the vinyl rolled up for about a day. When possible,

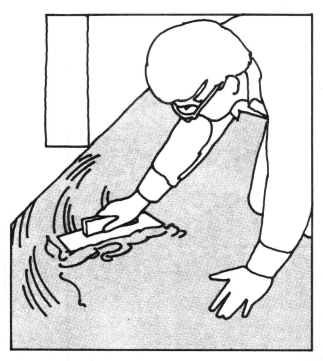

Illus. 17-2. Seal flooring cracks with flooring compound. Drawing courtesy of Georgia-Pacific Corp.

Illus. 17-3. Preliminary fit for vinyl sheet goods

maintain an even temperature of about 65 °F for the preparation period and installation.

Seams

Seams for vinyl are done differently than are those for carpet. If the flooring will need a seam, make the seam before installing the flooring. Lay the two pieces of flooring in place so that they overlap. Make sure the pattern of the floor meets and matches. Using a straightedge and a utility knife, cut through both pieces of flooring where the seam will be made. Remove the scrap flooring and attach the two pieces to the floor at the seam. Use a hand roller to press the flooring down on the adhesive or tape. Then, cover the seam with a sealing compound.

Laying Vinyl Flooring

When laying vinyl flooring, the vinyl should be laid out in the room with enough excess vinyl that the flooring rolls up on the walls (Illustrations 17-3 and 17-4). Use a utility knife to cut the vinyl (Illus. 17-5) where it must be fitted around corners. The vinyl

may be held in place by adhesive, tape, staples, or a combination of all of these.

Once the vinyl is in position, use a floor roller to roll out wrinkles. You can rent the necessary hand- and floor-rollers at tool-rental outlets. When the vinyl is flat, cut away the excess flooring. The utility knife can be run along a straightedge to cut the vinyl where it meets the walls. Baseboard or shoe moulding should then be installed to hide the joint between the floor and the wall.

There are kits available to help you install vinyl flooring (Illus. 17-6); these kits contain information and tools to help you install your own flooring (Illus. 17-7 and Illus. 17-8).

When shopping for flooring, try to see a large section of the flooring on display. Choosing from small samples can be disappointing (Illus. 17-9). A finished floor can look much different from the small sample

Illus. 17-4. Leave excess when laying vinyl flooring. Photo by the makers of Armstrong vinyl flooring

you saw in a showroom. If you prefer to work with individual vinyl squares, instead of sheet goods, there's an ample selection of good-quality vinyl tiles available (Illus. 17-10 and Illus. 17-11).

Use vinyl tiles to create your own designs (Illus. 17-12). Sheet vinyl can be purchased with designs imprinted into the vinyl (Illus. 17-13). If you prefer a uniform style without designs (Illus. 17-14), there are many styles to choose from.

Ceramic Tile

Ceramic tile is often found in bathrooms and kitchens. There are many different types and styles to choose from. There are also a number of ways to install tile floorings. Here are the most common ways.

Materials
Material for a tile floor can consist of quarry tile, mosaic tile, or glazed ceramic tile.

Illus. 17-5. Cutting vinyl flooring with a utility knife. Photo by the makers of Armstrong vinyl flooring

Quarry tile (Illus. 17-15) is big, and it comes in natural clay colors. Mosaic tile (Illus. 17-16) is small and generally comes with numerous tiles connected either to a backing or to a sheet of paper. The mosaic tile is placed on the paper (or the backing) in a pattern, and each pattern usually covers about one square foot. Glazed ceramic tile may have either a shiny finish or a matte finish. Ceramic tile may be bought as squares (Illus. 17-17) or rectangles. Sizes for ceramic tile vary from 4″ squares up to 6″ squares. Rectangular tile often comes in a dimension of approximately 4″ × 6″. Tile is available in a multitude of shapes.

Subfloor Conditions

Subfloor conditions are important for tile. Tile can be laid on either concrete or wood. When applying tile to wood subfloors, the subfloor should be covered with an under-layment, which should be at least ⅜″ thick and should be installed with ⅛″ expansion gaps between the sheets. If a concrete floor is in bad shape, fill cracks (Illus. 17-18) and level the floor with a mortar mix. Allow the mortar to cure before laying tile.

Bedding the Tile

The most common way to bed the tile is to set it into an adhesive (Illus. 17-19). For a

Illus. 17-6. Vinyl flooring installation kit. Photo by the makers of Armstrong vinyl flooring

wood subfloor, the adhesive may be either organic or epoxy. If the surface where the tile will be installed is damp, use an epoxy adhesive. When laying tile on concrete, use a bond coat of mortar or adhesive. An older method of bedding tile is the deep-set method. This requires a bed of mortar, about 1″ thick, to be put on the subfloor. Then, another bed of mortar is applied to the first, to hold the tile. The deep-set method adds considerable weight to the floor and has been replaced (mainly) with thin-set adhesives. The choice of adhesive is often determined by the manufacturer's recommendation and by the location and use of the tile. Check with your tile dealer for specifics.

Grout

Grout is the material placed between tiles to prevent water and dirt from collecting there (Illus. 17-20). There are many types of grout, and selecting the proper grout will depend upon the tile and the conditions of the installation. Check with your tile dealer before selecting the proper grout.

Illus. 17-7. Flooring knife. Photo by the makers of Armstrong vinyl flooring

Cutting & Installing Tile

Methods for cutting and installing tile are determined by the type of tile used and the conditions of the installation. Planning is a key element to good tile installation. Laying out the tile to obtain the proper pattern and spacing tiles evenly will take some thought. Tile cutters (Illus. 17-21) can be rented at tool-rental outlets. Some tile dealers will loan you tile cutters when you purchase tile from them. A rod saw can be used to cut most tiles (Illus. 17-22). Tile nippers are used to make small cuts on tile (Illus. 17-23).

Installation methods vary, so check with the dealer and follow the manufacturer's recommendations for tile installation. Here's one example of how to install tile:

Once you've planned the layout, trowel adhesive on the subfloor (Illus. 17-24). Generally, the adhesive should be ¼" thick. You can purchase plastic spacers to help you maintain even spacing between tiles. The spacers are cross-shaped, and they fit between the tiles. Lay your first tile in the center of the floor and lay all subsequent tiles from that point.

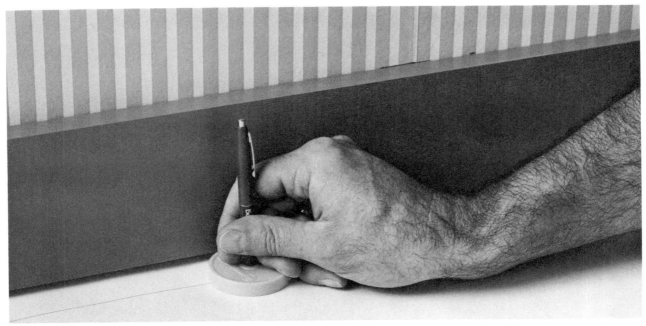

Illus. 17-8. Roller marker. Photo by the makers of Armstrong vinyl flooring

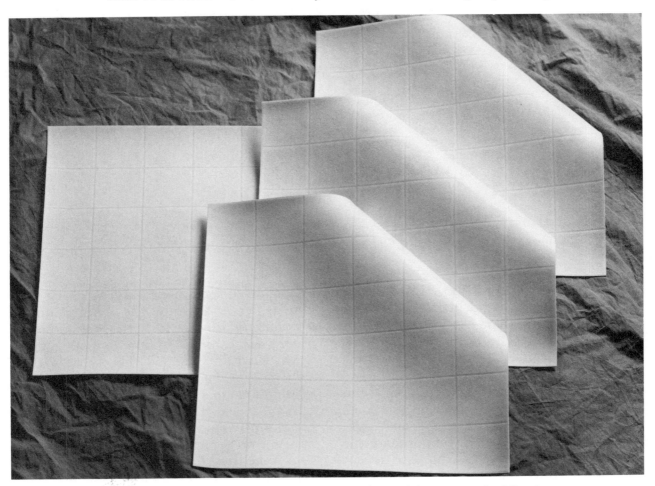

Illus. 17-9. Vinyl samples. Photo by the makers of Armstrong vinyl flooring

Illus. 17-10. Large vinyl tiles. Photo by the makers of Armstrong vinyl flooring

Illus. 17-11. Small vinyl tiles. Photo by the makers of Armstrong vinyl flooring

Illus. 17-12. Vinyl tile design. Photo by the makers of Armstrong vinyl flooring

Illus. 17-13. Sheet vinyl design. Photo by the makers of Armstrong vinyl flooring

Illus. 17-14. Uniform sheet vinyl flooring. Photo by the makers of Armstrong vinyl flooring

Illus. 17-15. Quarry tile. Art courtesy of Dal-Tile Corp.

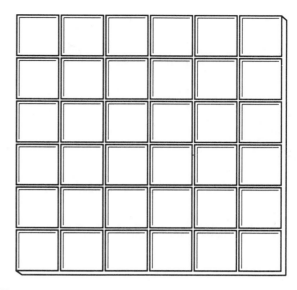

Illus. 17-16. Mosaic tile. Art courtesy of Dal-Tile Corp.

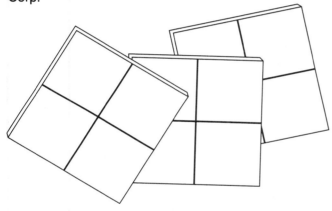

Illus. 17-17. Square tile. Art courtesy of Dal-Tile Corp.

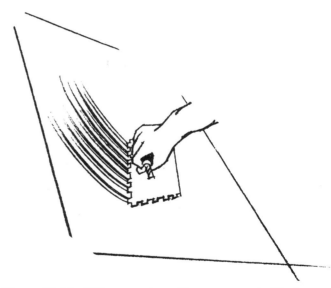

Illus. 17-18. Filling cracks with compound. Photo by the makers of Armstrong ceramic tile

Illus. 17-19. Setting tile in adhesive. Art courtesy of Dal-Tile Corp.

Illus. 17-20. Grouting tile. Photo by the makers of Armstrong ceramic tile

Illus. 17-21. Tile cutter. Photo by the makers of Armstrong ceramic tile

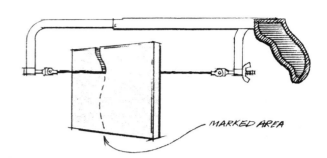

Illus. 17-22. Rod saw. Photo by the makers of Armstrong ceramic tile

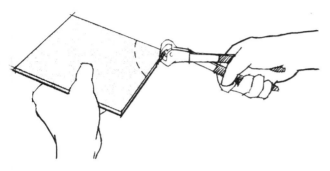

Illus. 17-23. Tile nippers. Photo by the makers of Armstrong ceramic tile

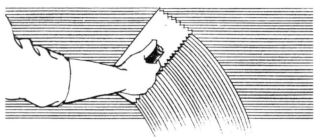

Illus. 17-24. Spreading adhesive on subfloor. Photo by the makers of Armstrong ceramic tile

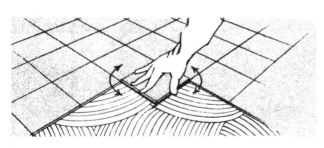

Illus. 17-25. Pressing and setting tile. Photo by the makers of Armstrong ceramic tile

Illus. 17-26. Using a wooden block and hammer to set tile. Photo by the makers of Armstrong ceramic tile

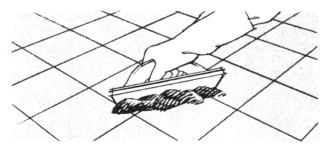

Illus. 17-27. Spreading grout material. Photo by the makers of Armstrong ceramic tile

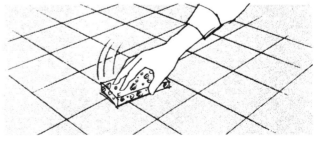

Illus. 17-28. Removing excess grout with a wet sponge. Photo by the makers of Armstrong ceramic tile

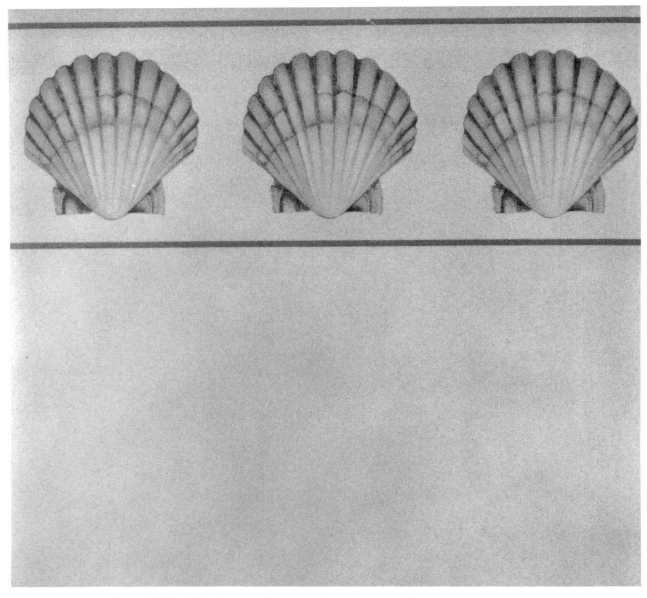

Illus. 17-29. Tile design. Photo by the makers of Armstrong ceramic tile

Set the tile into the adhesive, pressing firmly (Illus. 17-25). Sometimes rubber hammers are used to tap the tile in. A regular hammer can be used if you lay a block of wood over the tile and tap on the wooden block (Illus. 17-26). Use a long level to check the floor for consistency. Once all the tile is set, wait for the next step. How long you must wait is determined by the type of adhesive being used, so check the manufacturer's recommendations.

After waiting, you'll be ready to grout the tile. Check with your local tile dealer for the best type of grout to use with your tile, and follow the grout manufacturer's recommendations. In general, grout is mixed and spread over the floor, filling the gaps in the tile (Illus. 17-27). Grout is usually applied with a special trowel. Once the grout has filled the cracks, wash off the remainder of the grout with a wet sponge (Illus. 17-28). It will probably be necessary to wet the grout

Illus. 17-30. Design tile installed. Photo by the makers of Armstrong ceramic tile

Illus. 17-31. Black and white checkerboard design. Photo by the makers of Armstrong ceramic tile

Illus. 17-32. Tile with diamond accents. Photo by the makers of Armstrong ceramic tile

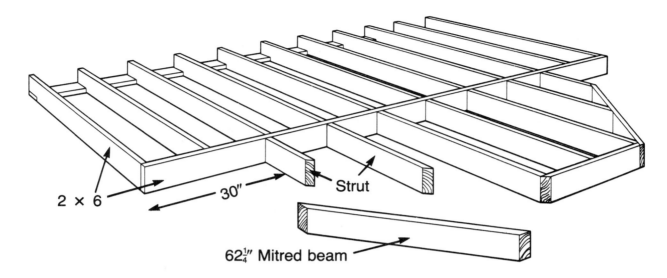

Illus. 17-33. Sleeper-floor system. Drawing courtesy of Georgia-Pacific Corp.

during the following three days to allow it to set properly.

Ceramic tile can give your new space many different looks. You can buy tile with designs (Illus. 17-29 and Illus. 17-30), or you might consider a black-and-white checkerboard look (Illus. 17-31), or you might consider diamond accents (Illus. 17-32).

Hardwood Flooring

Hardwood flooring is expensive, but attractive. Once common, hardwood floors are now found only in expensive housing. This type of flooring is generally narrow tongue-and-groove; special tools make the installation easy. However, you could also use wide wood planks or small wood squares. There are many types and grades of hardwood flooring. Talk with your local supplier, and ask to see samples before buying.

Subfloors
Subfloors of hardwood flooring can be made of plywood, boards, or sleeper joists. In most cases the subfloor will be plywood, at least ½″ thick. It's important to have the subfloor nailed tightly. Leave about ⅛″ between the

plywood sheets. You can use nails driven into the joists as temporary spacers.

If you want to install hardwood flooring over a concrete slab, consider moisture problems. If water or extreme dampness seeps up through the concrete, hardwood can warp and discolor. Even if you don't anticipate moisture problems, install a vapor barrier on the slab. The vapor barrier can be four-mil plastic.

Install the plastic vapor barrier on the slab and then lay sheets of exterior-grade plywood (as a subfloor) on the plastic. Powder-actuated nailing tools will make quick work of nailing the plywood to the concrete. If you use a sleeper system (Illus. 17-33), install the sleepers on the concrete and drape the plastic over the strips of wood (Illus. 17-34). If you install wood squares (similar to tile), you'll still need to cover the sleepers with plywood. But, for planks and tongue-and-groove strips, you can eliminate the plywood.

Tongue-and-Groove Flooring
Tongue-and-groove flooring (Illus. 17-35) is usually sold in narrow strips, ranging from 1½″ wide to just over 3″ wide, and usually about ¾″ thick. The length of strip flooring can range from 9″ to over 8′.

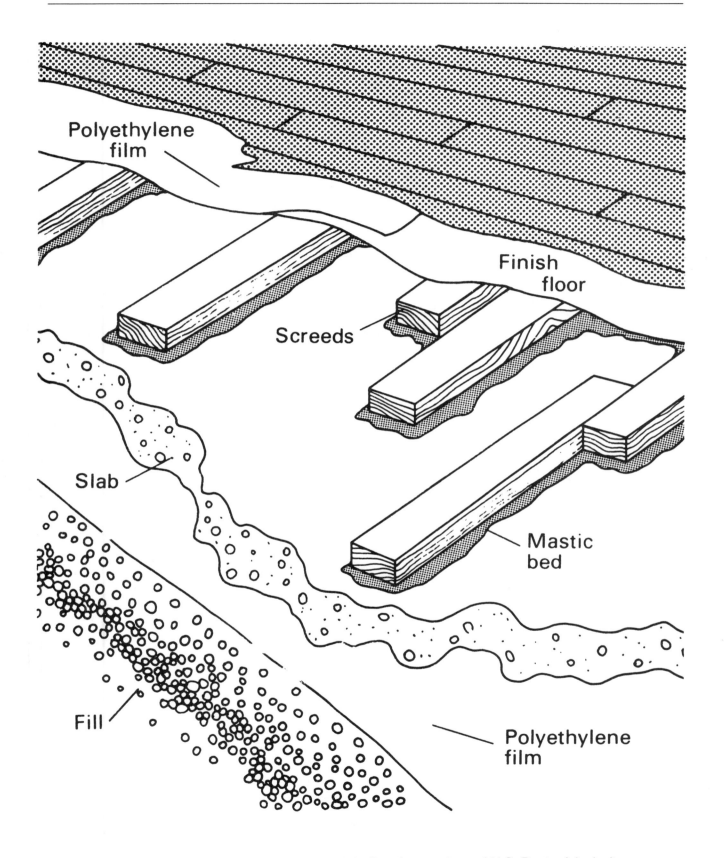

Illus. 17-34. Installing wood floors on a slab. Drawing courtesy of U.S. Dept. of Agriculture

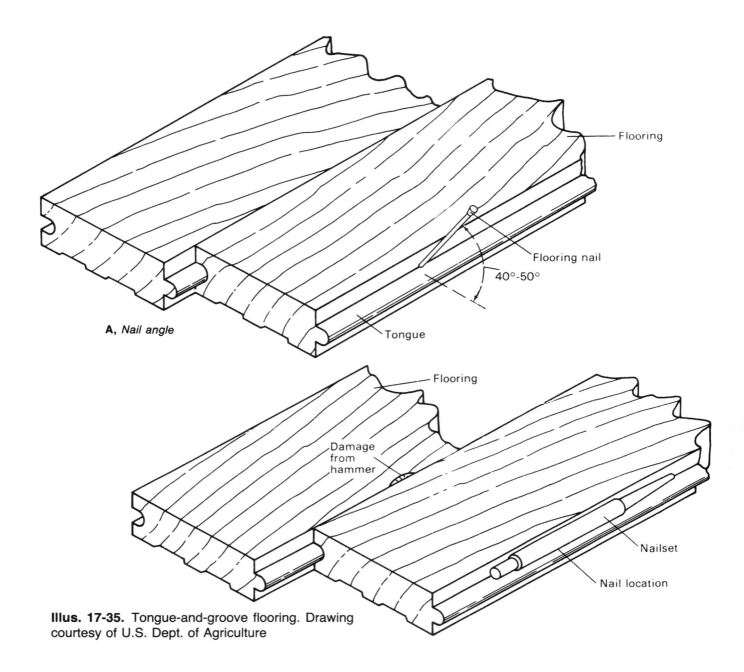

A, *Nail angle*

- Flooring
- Flooring nail
- 40°-50°
- Tongue
- Flooring
- Damage from hammer
- Nailset
- Nail location

Illus. 17-35. Tongue-and-groove flooring. Drawing courtesy of U.S. Dept. of Agriculture

Plank Flooring

Plank flooring generally isn't tongue-and-groove, but it can be. This type of wood floor is usually about ¾″ thick, and from 3″ to 8″ wide.

Flooring Squares

Flooring squares are wood-flooring material that resembles tile. The squares may be between 10″ to 36″ square. Rectangular shapes are also available. These hardwood tiles are generally installed with the use of an adhesive, in a fashion similar to that used in tile installation.

Finish

Hardwood flooring is commonly available already finished. This may cost a little more, but for the average person a prefinished floor is a bargain in terms of labor saved. If you prefer to do your own sanding and finishing, unfinished flooring is also available.

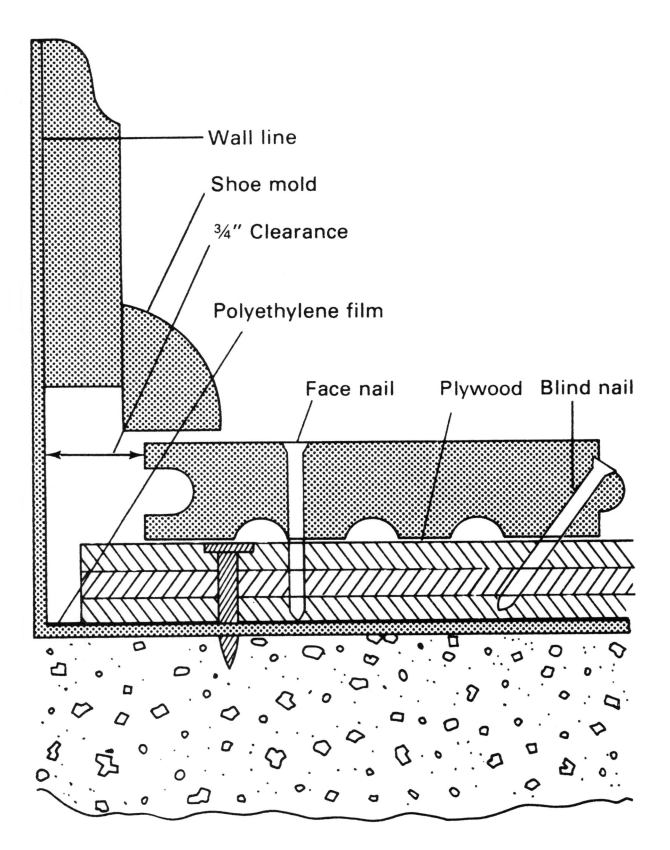

Wall line

Shoe mold

¾″ Clearance

Polyethylene film

Face nail   Plywood   Blind nail

Illus. 17-36. Nailing detail for wood floors. Drawing courtesy of U.S. Dept. of Agriculture

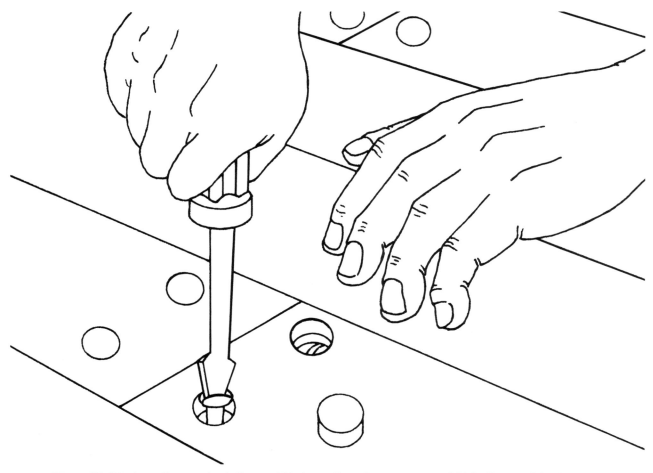

Illus. 17-37. Installing a plank floor with plugs. Drawing courtesy of U.S. Dept. of Agriculture

Nailing

Nailing down hardwood flooring using a hammer and nails can get fatiguing. Tool-rental outlets provide nailing devices that make flooring installation much easier. The nailer will drive nails in at an angle, keeping them concealed from view (Illus. 17-36). There's no need to predrill holes in the flooring when you use a nailing device. If you use a hammer and nails, predrill the nail holes.

The first strips of hardwood flooring are nailed from the top. Shoe moulding will hide the nail holes. Predrill the holes and nail the first strip to the subfloor. The grooved portion of the tongue-and-groove strip should be facing the wall. As the strips are installed, they're normally laid out in random lengths.

Nailing a plank flooring calls for different techniques. The planking will probably come with plugs to fill nail holes. If it doesn't, you will need a plug-cutter for your electric drill. Plank flooring is often installed with the use of recessed screws. Once the screws are in place, the wooden plugs are put in the holes to hide the screws (Illus. 17-37).

You Choose

There are many considerations and possible pitfalls to doing your own flooring. Carefully weigh the advantages against the potential disadvantages. If you feel confident about doing the job, do it. If you think you may be getting in over your head, don't feel embarrassed if you call in a pro.

18
Setting Fixtures

Setting fixtures is one of the last aspects of your job. Just because you're nearing the end, don't let your guard down. It's not uncommon for fixtures to be broken, floors to be damaged, or injuries to occur during this phase of work. Most of the fixture work will involve light and plumbing fixtures, but heating units may also come into play.

Plumbing Fixtures

Plumbing fixtures are generally easy to install, but they can pose some problems. Let's look at each common household fixture to determine the proper method of installation.

Toilets

Professionals can assemble and set a new toilet in less than 15 minutes. If the rough-in is right, the job is easy. The first step is to install the closet flange, if it wasn't installed already during the rough-in. Closet flanges should generally rest on the subfloor. If you'll be using thick floor tile, you may need to shim the flange to raise it above the subfloor. The top of the flange should never be below the finished floor.

With plastic pipe, the flange is glued into place. When setting the flange, be sure the grooves that will hold the closet bolts are in proper alignment. With most toilets the closet bolts should be set so that they are about 12″ from the back wall. After the flange is installed, place the closet bolt under the grooved lips of the flange. Next, place a wax ring over the opening in the flange. The wax should be installed at room temperature. If the wax is too cold, it won't seal well. If necessary, warm the wax under a light, with a heater, or (carefully) with a flame, before installing it.

Once the closet bolts and the wax ring are in place, set the bowl of the toilet onto the flange. The closet bolts should penetrate the holes in the base of the toilet. Push down on the toilet bowl. It may be necessary to straddle and sit on the bowl, facing the back wall, to have it seat and compress the wax properly.

Measure from the back wall to the holes in the toilet where the seat will be installed.

The two holes should be an equal distance from the back wall. If they aren't, twist the toilet bowl until both holes are the same distance from the back wall.

Install the flat plastic caps (they came with the toilet) over the closet bolts. If metal washers were packed with the closet bolts, install them next. Then, screw the nuts that came with the closet bolts onto the bolts. Use an adjustable wrench to tighten these nuts. Be careful when tightening the nuts, since toilet bases are fragile and will break if too much stress is applied to them. You'll know that these bolts are tight enough when the toilet can't shift from side to side. Snap the plastic cover caps (they came with the toilet) over the bolts and onto the flat plastic discs you installed over the bolts. If the bolts are too long to allow the caps to seat, cut down the bolts with a hacksaw.

Uncrate the toilet tank, and lay it on its back. Place the large sponge washer over the threaded piece that extends from the bottom of the tank; this piece is the base of the flush valve. Next, install the tank-to-bowl bolts. Most toilets are set up to accept two tank-to-bowl bolts, but some are designed to accept three bolts.

Slide the heavy black washers up over the bolts until they reach the heads. Push the bolts through the toilet tank. Now, pick up the tank and set it in place on the bowl. The sponge gasket and bolts should line up with the holes in the bowl. If you have one, ask your helper to hold the tank while you tighten the bolts. If you don't have a helper, be careful not to allow the tank to fall and break.

Once the tank is in place, slide the metal washers over the tank-to-bowl bolts from beneath the bowl. Follow the washers with nuts and tighten them. Again, be careful, since too much stress will crack the tank. Alternate between bolts as you tighten them. This allows the pressure to be applied evenly, reducing the chance of accidental breakage. Tighten these bolts until the tank is mounted firmly on the bowl.

Your next task is to connect the water supply to the toilet. The following example is based on the use of copper tubing for water distribution piping. If you used CPVC or some other type of pipe, use normal installation methods to install the cutoff valve. Cutoff valves for fixtures are normally called "stops."

First, make sure the water to the supply pipe is turned off. Then, cut off the supply pipe about ¾" above the floor or past the wall. Slide an escutcheon over the pipe. You could use stops that are held in place with soldered joints, but compression stops are easier and faster. Loosen the big nut on the compression stop and slide the stop onto the pipe. Use two adjustable wrenches to tighten the large nut. One wrench should be on the stop and the other should be on the large nut.

The next item you'll need is a closet supply. You can use a chrome supply, but polybutylene supplies are much easier to work with. In either case, remove the ballcock nut from the water-supply connection at the bottom of the toilet tank. Place the head of the closet supply on the ballcock supply and bend the supply to a point where it will fit in the supply opening of the stop. Mark the supply tube and cut it, either with roller-cutters (Illus. 18-1) or with a hacksaw.

Slide the ballcock nut onto the supply tube, with the threads facing the toilet tank. Slide the small nut from the stop onto the supply tube and follow it with the compression ferrule. If you use PB supply, use a nylon ferrule. Hold the supply up to the ballcock and tighten the ballcock nut. Insert the other end of the supply into the stop. Slide the ferrule down to the stop and tighten the small compression nut. Then, tighten the large ballcock nut.

Take the toilet seat from its box and install it. The seat will have built-in bolts that fit through holes in the bowl. Put the seat in place and tighten the nuts that hold it there.

Turn the handle of the stop clockwise until it stops, closing the valve. Turn on the main water supply. Open the stop valve by turning it counterclockwise. The toilet tank should fill with water. Once the tank is full, flush the toilet. Check around the base of the

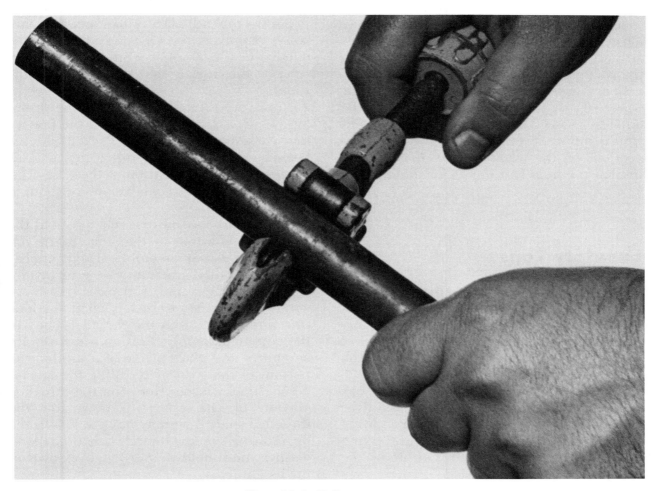

Illus. 18-1. Roller cutters

Illus. 18-2. Basin wrench

toilet for water. If water is present, you may have to pull and reset the toilet. Water around the base indicates a bad seal with the wax ring.

Check around the tank-to-bowl bolts for water. If you find any, gently tighten the nuts on these bolts, and the water should stop dripping. Check the compression connections on the water supply. If they leak, tighten the nuts and the leak should cease.

Lavatory Tops

Lavatory tops (with the lavatory bowl built into the top) rest on vanity cabinets. Normally, the tops are heavy enough to simply rest in place on the vanity, but you may have to set a smaller top in a bed of adhesive on the cabinet.

Once the top is set, you'll be ready to hook up the lavatory. Many plumbers mount the lavatory faucets on the bowl before setting the top. That's faster and easier than trying to do the job while scrunched up under the cabinet.

Some faucets come with a gasket that fits between the base of the faucet and the lavatory. If your faucet doesn't have such a gasket, make one from plumber's putty. Roll the putty into a long round line and place it around the perimeter of the faucet base. Set the faucet on the top, with the threaded fittings going through the holes.

Remove the supply nuts from the ends of the threaded fittings. Slide the ridged washers over the threaded fittings of the faucet. Then, screw on the mounting nuts. Tighten these nuts until the faucet won't twist about on the vanity top. Take two sink supply tubes and mount them to the bottom of the threaded fittings by sliding the supply nuts up the supply tubes and screwing the nuts onto the threaded fittings. The bevelled fit will prevent leaks. If you're working from inside the vanity, you'll need a basin wrench (Illus. 18-2) to tighten the mounting and supply nuts (Illus. 18-3).

Set the top into place. Make sure the main water supply is turned off, and install the cutoffs for the lavatory. Connect the supply tubes to the stops in the same way as for the toilet.

Now you're ready to connect the drainage. First, assemble and install the pop-up drain assembly (Illus. 18-4). Packed with the faucets, there will be detailed instructions for the proper installation of these devices. Here's a general idea of what you're about to do:

The pop-up assembly is what goes in the hole in the bottom of the sink. When you look at the pop-up assembly, it may appear confusing, but it's actually easy to install.

Unscrew the round trim piece (the piece you're accustomed to seeing when you look into a lavatory) from the threaded body of the pop-up assembly. Roll up some plumber's putty and place a ring of it around the bottom of the trim piece. Slide the fat, tapered, black washer that's on the threaded portion of the assembly down on the threaded shaft. You may have to loosen the big nut that's on the threads to get the metal washer and rubber washer to move down on the assembly.

Apply pipe dope, joint compound, or a sealant tape to the threads of the pop-up assembly. With your hand under the lavatory bowl, push the threaded assembly up through the drainage hole. Screw the small trim piece (the one with the putty on it) onto the threads. Push the tapered gasket up to the bottom of the lavatory. Tighten the mounting nut until it pushes the metal washer up to the rubber washer and compresses the rubber washer. You should notice putty being squeezed out from under the trim ring as you tighten the nut.

When the mounting nut is tight, the metal pop-up rod that extends from the assembly should be pointing to the rear of the lavatory bowl. Take the thin metal rod (the rod used to open and close the lavatory drain) and push it through the small hole in the middle of the faucet.

You should see a thin metal clip on the end of the rod that extends from the pop-up

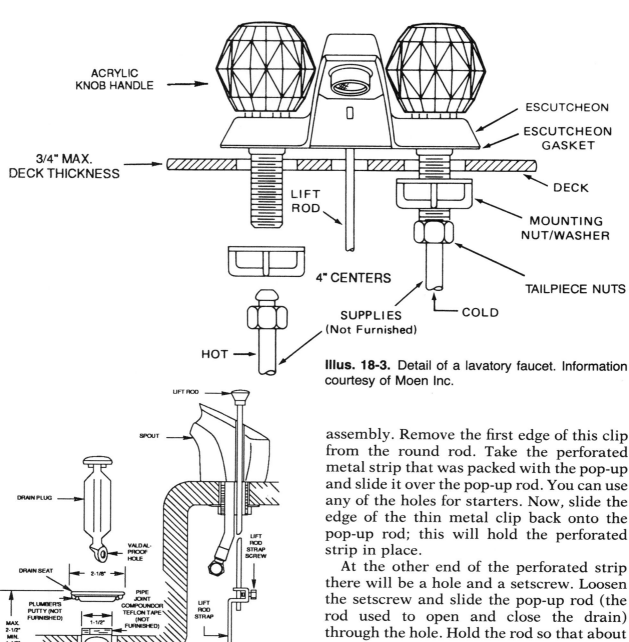

ACRYLIC
KNOB HANDLE →

ESCUTCHEON

ESCUTCHEON
GASKET

3/4" MAX.
DECK THICKNESS →

DECK

LIFT
ROD

MOUNTING
NUT/WASHER

TAILPIECE NUTS

4" CENTERS

SUPPLIES
(Not Furnished)

COLD

HOT →

Illus. 18-3. Detail of a lavatory faucet. Information courtesy of Moen Inc.

LIFT ROD →

SPOUT →

DRAIN PLUG →

VALDAL-
PROOF HOLE

LIFT
ROD
STRAP
SCREW

DRAIN SEAT

2-1/8"

PIPE
JOINT
COMPOUND OR
TEFLON TAPE
(NOT
FURNISHED)

LIFT
ROD
STRAP

PLUMBERS
PUTTY (NOT
FURNISHED)

1-1/2"

MAX.
2-1/2"
MIN.
1-1/2"

BOTTOM
GASKET

FLAT
WASHER

SPRING
CLIP

MOUNTING
NUT

DRAIN
BODY

8"

PIVOT
NUT

PIVOT ROD SEAT
(NOT SHOWN)

PIPE
JOINT
COMPOUND
OR TEFLON TAPE
(NOT
FURNISHED)

1-1/4"

LIFT ROD
STRAP
SHOWN IN
BENT
POSITION

PIVOT
ROD
(DOWN
POSITION)

TAILPIPE

Illus. 18-4. Pop-up assembly. Information courtesy of Moen Inc.

assembly. Remove the first edge of this clip from the round rod. Take the perforated metal strip that was packed with the pop-up and slide it over the pop-up rod. You can use any of the holes for starters. Now, slide the edge of the thin metal clip back onto the pop-up rod; this will hold the perforated strip in place.

At the other end of the perforated strip there will be a hole and a setscrew. Loosen the setscrew and slide the pop-up rod (the rod used to open and close the drain) through the hole. Hold the rod so that about 1½″ protrude above the top of the faucet. Tighten the setscrew. Pull up on the pop-rod and see that it operates the pop-up plug (the stopper in the sink drain). You can test this best after all connections are made to the water and drainage systems.

There should be a 1¼″ chrome tailpiece (a round tubular piece) that was packed with the pop-up assembly. The tailpiece will have fine threads on one end and no threads on the other. Coat the threads with pipe dope or sealant tape. Screw the tailpiece into the bottom of the pop-up assembly.

Now you'll be ready to install the trap. First, slide an escutcheon over the trap arm (Illus. 18-5) (the piece of pipe stubbed out for the trap). Lavatory traps are normally 1¼", but you can use a 1½" trap with a reducing nut on the end that connects to the tailpiece. Assuming you used plastic pipe for the rough-in, you may glue the trap directly to the trap arm (if you're using a schedule-40 trap), or you could use a trap adapter, if you're using a metal trap. Trap adapters glue onto pipe just like any other fitting. One end of the adapter is equipped with threads to accept a slip-nut.

Start by placing the trap on the tailpiece. To do this, remove the slip-nut from the vertical section of the trap. Slide the slip nut onto the tailpiece and follow it with the washer that was under it. The washer may be nylon or rubber. Put the trap on the tailpiece and check the alignment with the trap arm. It may be necessary to use a fitting to offset the trap arm in the direction of the trap.

If the trap is below the trap arm, you'll have to shorten the tailpiece. The tailpiece is best cut with a pair of roller-cutters, but it can be cut with a hacksaw. You may have to remove the tailpiece to cut it. If the trap is too low, you can use a tailpiece extension to reach it. A tailpiece extension is a tubular section that fits between the trap and the tailpiece. The extension may be plastic or metal, and it's held in place with slip-nuts and washers.

Once the trap is at the proper height, you must determine if the trap arm needs to be cut or extended. Extending the trap arm can be done with a regular coupling and pipe section. If you're using a schedule-40 plastic trap, it's glued onto the trap arm. If you're using a metal trap, the long section of the trap will slip into a trap adapter. You may have to shorten the length of the trap's horizontal section. When using a trap adapter, slide the slip-nut and washer onto the trap section. Then, insert the trap section into the adapter and secure it by tightening the slip-nut. Once the trap-to-trap-arm connection is

Illus. 18-5. Chrome P-trap

complete, tighten the slip-nut at the tailpiece.

Your next job is to install the cutoffs. To accomplish this, use the same procedures described in the section on toilets. Make sure the main water supply is turned off. Cut the pipe stubs and install escutcheons. Install the stops and connect the supply tubes to the stops. Make sure the stops are in the "off" position, and turn the main water supply back on.

Remove the aerator (the piece that screws into or onto the faucet spout) from the faucet. If you don't remove the aerator, it may become blocked with debris and cause an erratic water stream. Make sure the faucet is turned off, and open the stops. Close the lavatory drain by pulling up the pop-up rod. Turn on the left-hand faucet and make sure it produces hot water. Hot should always be on the left and cold should always be on the right. If for some reason you roughed your pipes in on the wrong sides, you can correct the mistake by using long supply tubes and crossing them under the lavatory.

Fill the lavatory with water. If the bowl won't hold the water, adjust the pop-up controls. Getting the pop-up set in the right holes and at the proper height may take experimentation. Release the water in the bowl and check all drainage fittings for leaks. If there are leaks at slip-nuts, tightening the nuts should solve the problem. If you have a leak at a threaded connection, try tightening the threads, but you may have to remove the piece and install additional pipe dope or tape.

Drop-In Lavatories

Drop-in lavatories differ from other lavatories only in the way the bowl is installed. The waste and water connections for all lavatories are essentially the same. Drop-in lavatories are so named because the bowl simply drops into a countertop. A hole is cut in the top that is slightly smaller than the rim diameter of the lavatory. Caulking is applied around the edge of the hole, on the top

of the counter. The drop-in lavatory is set into place and connected to the drain and water supply. There are no special mounting brackets or clips; the weight of the lavatory holds it in place.

Rimmed Lavatories

Rimmed lavatories aren't very popular. These lavatories have a metal ring surrounding them that collects dirt and is hard to clean. Installing a rimmed lavatory requires cutting a hole in the countertop, using a template supplied with the lavatory. The metal ring is set in the hole. Then, the lavatory is installed from below the countertop. The bowl is held up from below until it comes into contact with the ring. Special clips are used to hold the bowl in place. The clips fit in a channel that runs around the metal ring. As the clips are tightened, they apply pressure on the bottom of the lavatory rim. These lavatories can be difficult to install, especially without help.

Illus. 18-6. Tub shower detail. Information courtesy of Moen Inc.

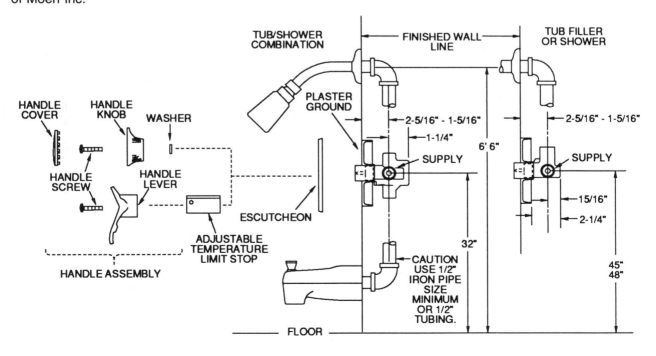

Wall-Hung Lavatories

Wall-hung lavatories hang on a wall bracket. When wall-hung lavatories will be used, wood backing must be installed during the rough-in phase. The backing, a 2 × 8, is nailed between two studs. The backing provides a solid place to install the screws that will support the wall bracket.

In the trim-out phase, the wall bracket is hung and secured with screws or lag bolts. The directions that come with wall-hung lavatories should give the proper height for the bracket. The top of the bracket will normally be about 30″ or 31″ above the floor. As you secure the bracket, make sure it stays level.

Once the bracket is installed, the lavatory is placed on the bracket. Be sure the lavatory is seated firmly on the bracket; if the bowl falls, it may break. Once it's on the bracket, check that the bowl is level. You may have to use the heel of your hand to tap the lavatory down on one end or the other until it's level.

Some (but not all) wall-hung units have holes in them for additional lag bolts. These holes allow lag bolts to be run through the lavatory after it is on the bracket, ensuring that it won't be knocked off the bracket.

Tub & Shower Trim

The tub and shower trim for faucets is easy to install. However, installing a tub waste is difficult, unless you have help.

Shower Trim

Shower trim is easy to install. Start with the shower head. Be sure the main water supply is turned off, and unscrew the stub-out from the shower-head ell. Slide the escutcheon that came with the shower assembly over the shower arm. Apply pipe dope or tape to the threads on each end of the shower arm. Screw the shower head on the short section of the arm, where the bend is. Screw the long section of the arm into the threaded ell in the wall.

Use an adjustable wrench on the flats around the shower head to tighten all connections. If you must use pliers on the arm, keep them close to the wall, so that the escutcheon will hide scratch marks.

Now you'll be ready to trim out the shower valve. How this is done will depend on the type of faucet you roughed in. Follow the manufacturer's suggestions. If you installed a single-handle unit, you'll normally install the large escutcheon first (Illus. 18-6). These escutcheons normally use a foam gasket, removing the need for plumber's putty. Then the handle is installed and the cover cap is snapped into place over the handle screw. If you are using a two-handle faucet, you will normally screw in chrome collars over the faucet stems. These may be followed by escutcheons, or the escutcheons may be an integral part of the sleeves. Putty should be placed where the escutcheons come into contact with the tub wall. Finally, the handles are installed.

Tub Faucets

Tub faucets are trimmed in the same way as shower faucets are. However, you'll have a tub spout to install. Some tub spouts slide over a piece of copper tubing and are held in place with a setscrew. Many tub spouts have a female-threaded connection, either at the inlet or the outlet of the spout. If there's a threaded connection, you must solder a male adapter onto the stub-out from your tub valve or use a threaded ell and galvanized nipple. The type of spout that slides over the copper tubing and attaches with a setscrew is by far the easiest to install. Place plumber's putty on the tub spout where it comes into contact with the tub wall.

Tub Wastes

Tub wastes are difficult to install if you're working alone. The tub waste and overflow can take several forms. It may be made of metal or plastic. It can use a trip lever, a push button, a twist-and-turn stopper, or an old-fashioned rubber stopper. The tub waste may go together with slip-nuts or glued joints. Follow the directions that come with your tub waste.

First, mount the drain (Illus. 18-7). Unscrew the chrome drain from the tub shoe. You'll see a thick black washer. Install a ring of putty around the chrome drain, and apply pipe dope to the threads. Hold (or have your assistant hold) the tub shoe under the tub so that it lines up with the drain hole. Screw the chrome drain into the female threads of the shoe. The black washer should be on the bottom of the tub, between the tub and the shoe. Once the chrome drain is tight, leave it alone for the time being.

The tub shoe has a tubular drainage pipe extending from it. Make this drain point towards the head of the tub, where the faucets are installed. Take the tee that came with the tub waste and put it on the drainage tube from the shoe. Then, take the long drainage tube (that will accept the tub's

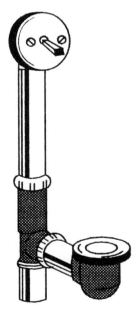

Illus. 18-7. Tub waste. Information courtesy of Moen Inc.

overflow) and place it in the top of the tee. You want the face of the overflow tube to line up with the overflow hole in the tub. Cut the tubing on the overflow or shoe tubing as needed. The cuts are best made with roller-cutters, but they can be made with a hacksaw.

You should have a sponge gasket in your assortment of parts. This gasket will be placed on the face of the overflow tubing, between the back of the tub and the overflow head. From inside the bathtub, install the faceplate for the overflow. For trip-lever styles, you will have to fish the trip mechanism down the overflow tubing. For other types of tub waste, you'll only have a cover plate to screw on. Tighten the screws until the sponge gasket is compressed.

Now, tighten the drain by crossing two large screwdrivers and using them between the crossbars of the drain. Turn the drain clockwise until the putty spreads out from under the drain. The last step is connecting the tub waste to the trap. This can be done with trap adapters or glue joints, depending upon the type of tub waste you've used.

Apply joint compound to the threads of the tailpiece (if you're using a metal waste) and screw the tailpiece into place. From there on, the process is just the same as that for hooking up a lavatory drain.

Kitchen Sinks

Kitchen sinks are similar to lavatories, but there are differences.

Mounting the Sink

Mounting the kitchen sink is normally done in one of two ways. Some kitchen sinks are drop-ins. Like lavatories, drop-in sinks don't require clips, only caulking. Most kitchen sinks, however, are held in place with clips. These clips slide into a channel that runs around the rim of the sink. As the clips are tightened (usually with a screwdriver), they bite into the bottom of the countertop, pulling the sink firmly into contact with the top of the counter. (See Illustrations 18-8 through 18-14.) There are different types of sink clamp, so check the materials and the manufacturer's instructions for proper installation. (See Illustrations 18-15 through 18-17.)

Basket Strainers

Instead of pop-up mechanisms, kitchen

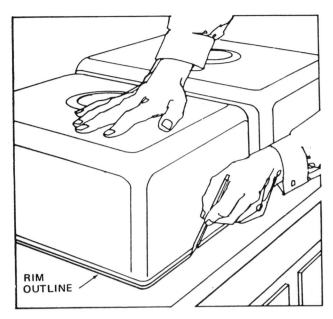

Illus. 18-8. Outline the rim of the sink. Information courtesy of Moen Inc.

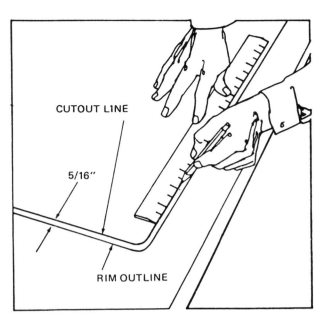

Illus. 18-9. Mark the cut line. Information courtesy of Moen Inc.

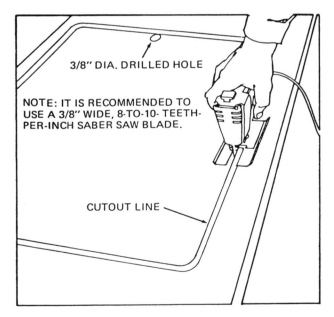

Illus. 18-10. Cut the counter to accept the sink. Information courtesy of Moen Inc.

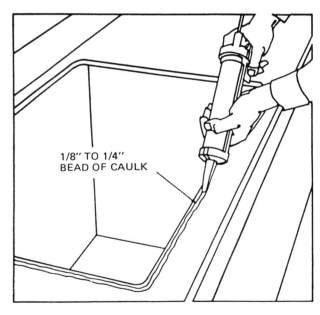

Illus. 18-11. Caulk around sink hole. Information courtesy of Moen Inc.

sinks use basket strainers for drains. Putty is applied around the rim of the drain and the drain is pushed through the hole in the sink. From below, a fibre gasket is slid over the threaded portion of the drain and a large nut is applied and tightened. These nuts can be difficult to tighten without help. Have an assistant cross screwdrivers in the crossbars of the basket strainer as the nut is being tightened. Otherwise, the entire drain assembly tends to turn without tightening.

A good solution for someone who's work-

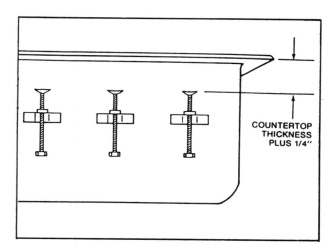

Illus. 18-12. Install clamps, depending upon the type of sink. Information courtesy of Moen Inc.

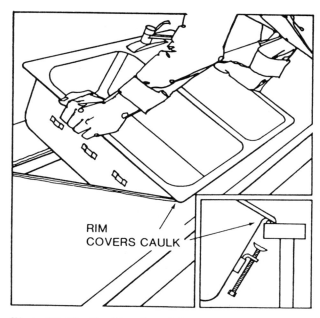

Illus. 18-13. Position the sink. Information courtesy of Moen Inc.

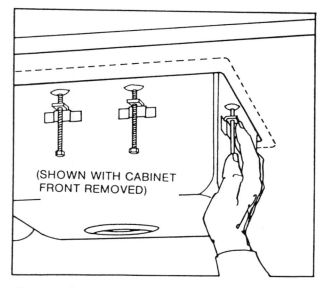

Illus. 18-14. Tighten sink clips. Information courtesy of Moen Inc.

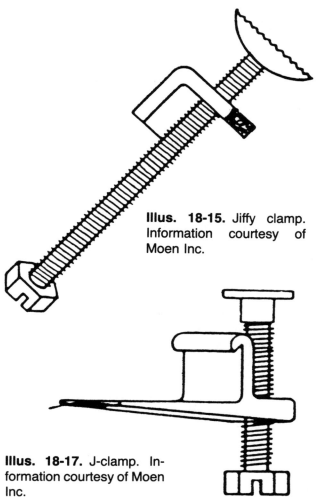

Illus. 18-15. Jiffy clamp. Information courtesy of Moen Inc.

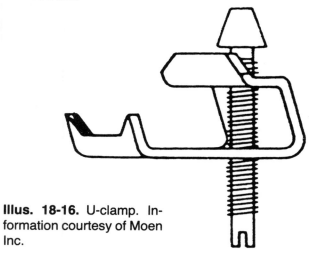

Illus. 18-16. U-clamp. Information courtesy of Moen Inc.

Illus. 18-17. J-clamp. Information courtesy of Moen Inc.

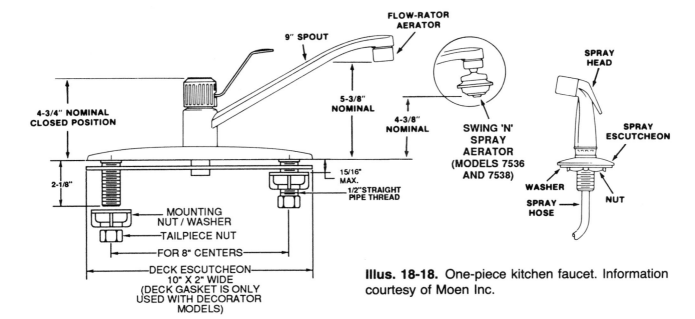

Illus. 18-18. One-piece kitchen faucet. Information courtesy of Moen Inc.

ing alone is a type of drain that uses a flange to secure the basket strainer. With this type of drain, the flange slides over the threads and is held against the bottom of the sink at three pressure points. The pressure points are threaded rods, extending from another flange that's screwed onto the drain threads. As the threaded rods are tightened, they apply pressure and seal the drain.

Tailpieces

Kitchen tailpieces don't screw into the basket strainers. Instead, they're flanged to accept tailpiece washers. The nylon washer sits atop the tailpiece, and the tailpiece is held in place with a slip-nut.

Continuous Wastes

Since many kitchen sinks have two bowls, continuous wastes are often used to drain the two bowls to a common trap. There are end-outlet wastes and center-outlet wastes. The continuous waste attaches to the sink's tailpieces with slip-nuts and washers. Then, the waste tubes run either to a tee, for an end-outlet waste, or to a double tee, for a center-outlet waste. The bottoms of these tees accept a tailpiece and allow the trap to be attached.

Garbage Disposers

Garbage disposers, mounted to the kitchen sink, take the place of basket strainers. Putty is applied to the ring of the disposer's trim piece. The trim is pushed through the drain hole. A pressure-type flange is put over the collar of the drain and followed by a snap ring. The snap ring holds the pressure flange in place. Threaded rods are tightened with a screwdriver to seal the drain. Then, the disposer is held into place: A rotating collar is turned to lock onto it.

The disposer has a small ell that comes with it. Two screws are loosened on the side of the disposer. The ell fits through a metal housing, and a rubber washer is placed on the bevelled end of the ell (the short end). The metal housing is put back in place and the screws are tightened. This compresses the gasket between the face of the ell and the side of the disposer. Then, the continuous waste or trap is connected to the bottom of the disposer ell.

Dishwashers

Dishwashers are normally installed under the countertop, between cabinets. There are metal tabs at the top of the dishwasher that allow screws to be installed to hold the appliance in place. A rubber drain hose connects to a ridged nylon drain on the appliance. The hose is held in place by a snap ring or clamp. This hose should run into the sink base and rise to the top of the enclosure. It should connect (with clamps) to an *air gap*.

An *air gap* is a device that rests on the counter and has a chrome cover. It's installed by removing the chrome cover and mounting nut. The unit is pushed up through its hole from beneath the counter. Then the gasket and mounting nut are installed and tightened. Afterwards, the chrome cover is replaced. Below the counter, the air gap splits off into a wye.

The small hose from the dishwasher connects to one side of the wye and is held in place with a clamp. Then, a larger hose is run from the other section of the wye to a wye-tailpiece connection, or a connection point on a disposer. If you're connecting to a disposer, you must knock out the factory-installed plug with a sturdy screwdriver and a hammer before connecting the hose. Knock out this plug before installing the disposer, or retrieving the knocked-out plug will be difficult.

To connect the water supply to the dishwasher, use a dishwasher stop or cut a tee into the hot-water supply to the sink. A dishwasher stop has provisions for a supply tube to the sink and for the tubing running to the dishwasher. The copper tubing for the dishwasher should be equipped with a cutoff valve. If you use a dishwasher stop, you have a built-in cutoff. If you cut in a tee, install a stop-and-waste valve between the tee and the dishwasher tubing.

The tubing will run to a point under the dishwasher. A dishwasher ell is used to make the connection between the tubing and the dishwasher. The dishwasher ell screws into the dishwasher. Use pipe dope or tape on the threads. The tubing connects to the ell with a compression nut and ferrule.

Bar Sinks

Bar sinks are miniature kitchen sinks. The installation procedures for both sinks are essentially the same.

Faucets

When selecting faucets, choose those that are all in one piece (Illus. 18-18). Some "designer" faucets come with handles and spout as individual units. For the homeowner, putting these delicate and sometimes intricate faucets together can be troublesome.

Heating Trim

Heating trim is relatively easy to install. In the case of a forced-air system, all you have to do is set registers into the ducts. Cut out the section of flooring that covers the duct opening and insert the register. Keep your flooring cuts smaller than the register. A mistake in sizing the register hole can cause considerable trouble.

With hot-water baseboard units, the trim work is complex, but still manageable. Hot-water heat generally consists of copper tubing with fins on it. You will have pipe stubs already roughed in. Turn off the water to the stubs and begin installation, which involves screwing the baseboard units to the wall and soldering the copper connection. Splicers, used for joining baseboard units in long runs, are merely trim pieces that hide the seam where two pieces of heat pipe butt together. End caps will be installed at each end of the heat pipe to hide valves, ells, and the exposed ends of heating elements.

If you install hot-water baseboard heat that has its own zone, you'll have to mount a thermostat. Thermostats are normally mounted chest-high, and they must be level to function properly. Some thermostats are set up for a two-wire system and others for a three-wire system. Buy a thermostat to match your wiring. The thermostat may be for a 24-volt system, or it could be for a 750-

millivolt system. Confirm your needs and make sure that the thermostat you purchase will work with your existing heating system.

When mounting the thermostat, remove the cover. The back of the unit is the mounting surface. You'll see holes in the back casing of the unit. Screw the base to the wall, making sure that it remains level. Connect wiring in accordance with the wiring diagram supplied with the equipment. Replace the cover, and you'll be done.

Electric baseboard heat will be connected electrically and then screwed to the wall. Remember to turn off the power when you work with wiring.

Electrical Fixtures & Devices

Electrical fixtures (generally lights) are not difficult to install, but do be cautious. Always be sure that the wires you're working with aren't "hot" with electricity.

Wiring Devices

When installing wiring devices (outlets and switches) be absolutely sure that the power is off at the circuits you're working with. Use a knife and a wire stripper to prepare the ends of the roughed-in wiring for the connection to devices. There's a color-code system that should be followed when installing electrical devices. Green wires or bare copper wires should be used as ground wires. Red wires should be considered hot wires; they usually attach to brass or chrome screws. Black wires are also considered hot and they generally attach to brass screws. In many cases, white wires serve as a neutral wire and connect to chrome screws, but don't count on white wires *not* being hot.

There are times when the white wires are used as black wire. Most electricians will wrap black tape around the white wire to indicate its use as a hot wire. However, never assume *anything* when working with electricity. If you have reason to use a white wire as a black wire, wrap it with black tape or tag it in some way to indicate its use.

Some receptacles are made to allow wires to be stuck into them (rather than placing the wires under screws). Most professionals frown on this practice, and they prefer to secure wires under screws. When you crook the end of wires to fit under screws, bend the wires so the crook will tighten as the screw is tightened. For example, as you're holding the wire, bend the crook so the end of the wire curls to your right.

When joining two wires to each other, use wire nuts. Wire nuts come in various sizes to fit different-size wires. The nuts have a plastic exterior and a metal spring on the inside. Twist the wires together before installing the wire nuts. Place the wire nut over the wires and turn the nut clockwise. As you turn the nut, the connection between the wires is secured with the spring, and the nut becomes attached tightly to the wires. Make sure all bare wiring is concealed in the wire nut.

Most metal electrical boxes will have a green screw for the ground wire to be mounted under. Some electricians use a ground clip. Ground clips are just thin metal clips that slide over the edge of a metal box and bring the ground wire into contact with the metal.

Plan on installing ground-fault receptacles or circuit breakers in bathrooms. Check your local code for the required location of the ground-fault interceptor (GFI) outlet.

Wall Plates & Switch Covers

Wall plates and switch covers are mounted over outlet boxes and switch boxes; they're held in place with screws.

Light Fixtures

Light fixtures aren't very difficult to install. Just match up the feed wires with the fixture wires and mount the fixture. Most fixtures will have threaded studs that hold them to their electrical box. Follow the directions that come packed with your light fixtures, and follow the manufacturer's recommendations.

19
Clean-Up & Punch-Out

Congratulations! Your job is *almost* finished. All that's left are the clean-up and punch-out. "Punch-out" work is adjustment and correction, and it might include adjusting the way a door shuts, touching up paint, or correcting minor plumbing leaks. Clean-up might include removing labels, construction debris, or anything else necessary to give the job a clean and neat appearance.

This final chapter concentrates on putting the finishing touches on your job. You'll learn how to remove the big black letters from your vinyl flooring; you'll be given tips for cleaning plumbing fixtures. In addition, you'll learn how to hide minor mistakes.

Walls & Ceilings

Walls and ceilings shouldn't need cleaning, but they may need some touch-up, since they may accumulate holes or scratches during the work. Here are some suggestions if you have minor imperfections to hide. Don't dab paint on a small area. The paint will be too heavy and it will show as a patch. Apply paint in a thin coat and feather it out to a larger area. By gradually feathering the paint, you'll hide the defect without drawing attention to it.

Floor Coverings

Vinyl flooring is usually imprinted with the manufacturer's name. These big black letters can seem intimidating, but common household cleansers mixed with warm water will wash the words away.

New carpet should be vacuumed several times before it's truly clean and in showroom condition. Vacuum *against* the grain to raise the pile of the carpet. In the beginning, vacuum in all directions to remove stray fibres and dirt.

Plumbing Fixtures

Plumbing fixtures are often covered with adhesive labels which stick very well and can be extremely difficult to remove. *Very* hot water will loosen the glue on the labels. Protect your hands from the hot water with heavy rubber gloves. If the stickers still won't come off, use a straight-edge razor blade, cautiously.

Even after removing the labels, you may have a sticky residue on the fixture, where the label once was. This residue can be removed with your fingernail, a razor blade, or a soft plastic scrubber, the kind used for washing dishes.

On a regular basis, and until the system has settled in (about two weeks), check all visible plumbing connections for leaks. Compression fittings frequently develop leaks during the first days of operation. Slip-nut connections are also prone to post-installation leaks. If they do leak, tighten the nuts and the leaks should stop.

Light Fixtures

Light fixtures can be cleaned with soft rags and window-washing solution. Be careful not to break the delicate glass.

Windows

Windows frequently carry manufacturers' labels. A straight-edge razor blade will remove these stubborn stickers. The razor blade will also make quick work of removing any unwanted paint from the glass.

Doors

Doors will occasionally need to be adjusted after the initial installation. If the door doesn't latch properly, check the position of the striker plate. If the door drags on the carpet, remove it from the hinges, and plane or cut the bottom of the door until it swings freely.

Hot-Water Heating Systems

If your new hot-water heating system isn't working, check for air locks. If air is trapped in the pipes, the hot water won't circulate properly. Open an air vent at the highest possible point and let air out of the system until water comes through the air vent. Close the vent and test the system; it should then produce heat.

Looking for Hidden Defects

Look for hidden defects by inspecting the work under both natural and artificial light. Imperfections that go unnoticed under one kind of light will often show up under the other. Imagine your embarrassment if you should invite people over to celebrate your new living space and the first thing visible when the lights are turned on is sloppy ceiling seams.

Go over your job carefully. Look for hidden defects. Make a list ("punch-list") of every item you discover that needs attention. Most people make a punch-list to give to their contractor for repairs. However, as a do-it-yourselfer, you are both consumer and contractor; you must fix your own imperfections.

Completing the Punch-List Items

Don't put off attending to the punch-list items. The longer you wait to correct deficiencies, the longer you'll be complacent enough to live with them. Fix problems and make adjustments as they're found. Procrastinating will only make the job more difficult.

With the right planning, execution, and clean-up, your new space should make you proud. Your choice in windows and doors will let light brighten your converted space and show it off. A wall of glass can transform your new attic bedroom into a suite you might never want to leave. Color plates Y and Z show some beautiful conversions.

Using that space in your garage or basement can give you an extra bedroom or an office (Illus. 19-1). A kitchen in the attic can be set off with quarry tile and a skylight (Illus. 19-2). A pedestal lavatory can add elegance to your new bathroom, and gold faucets can enhance the look of any vanity. These accessories are shown in the color section.

Chair rail, wallpaper, and good flooring will distinguish any room. Casement windows, skylights, and a spa will make your attic bathroom the most popular room in the house. Color-coordinated flooring, cabinets, and furnishings will make your new in-law quarters attractive and desirable. Adding a roof window to your new office will provide natural light and good ventilation. All of these ideas are pictured in the color section.

Illus. 19-1. Garage office. Photo courtesy of Lis King and Mark Parsons

Illus. 19-2. Attic kitchen. Photo courtesy of Quaker Maid, A Division of WCI, Inc.

Acknowledgments

I'd like to acknowledge and thank the following companies for assisting me in the illustration of this book:

Andersen Windows, Inc.
100 4th Ave. North
Bayport, MN 55003-1096

Armstrong World Industries, Inc.
P.O. Box 3001
Lancaster, PA 17604-3001

Dal-Tile
P.O. Box 17130
Dallas, TX 75217

Georgia-Pacific Corp.
P.O. Box 105605
Atlanta, GA 30348-5605

Mannington Resilient Floors
P.O. Box 30
Salem, NJ 08079-0030

Moen Inc.
377 Woodland Ave.
Elyria, OH 44036-2111

Morgan Manufacturing
P.O. Box 2446
Oshkosh, WI 54903-2446

NuTone, Inc.
Madison & Red Bank Roads
Cincinnati, OH 45227-1599

Quaker Maid, a Division of WCI, Inc.
Rt. 61, P.O. Box H
Leesport, PA 19533-9984

Ralph Wilson Plastics Co.
P.O. Box 6110
Temple, TX 76503-6110

Skymaster
P.O. Box 536925
Orlando, FL 32853-6925

Tub-Master
P.O. Box 536925
Orlando, FL 32853-6925

Velux-America, Inc.
P.O. Box 5001
Greenwood, SC 29648

Weil-McLain, a Division of the Marley Co.
Blaine St.
Michigan City, IN 46360

Wood-Mode, Inc.
One Second St.
Kreamer, PA 17833

Thanks also to Fran Pagurko, model.

This book is dedicated to my daughter, Afton Amber Woodson, and to my wife, Kimberley Woodson.

Glossary

Baluster: a vertical member of a stair railing, sometimes called a picket

Band board: a board that's nailed to the ends of floor joists, on the outside perimeter of a building

Baseboard: a trim board that's installed where a wall meets a floor

Bearing wall: a wall that supports the weight of other building components

Bird's mouth: a notch cut in a rafter to allow the rafter to rest on the top plate of an exterior wall

Bottom plate: a board (or a combination of boards) that forms the base of a wall

Bridging: metal or wooden members that are nailed diagonally between joists to prevent the joists from twisting

Butt joint: the joint where two flat ends of wood, or other objects, come together

Casing: moulding used to trim around windows and doors

Cleat: a strip of wood used to support an object (like a countertop)

Collar tie: a board nailed between two rafters, near the ridgeboard, to give added strength to the roof

Corner board: a trim board placed on the outside of a building that gives siding a place to butt into, at the corners

Cornice: the overhang of a pitched roof at the eave line

Dead load: the weight of the components comprising the construction of a building

Dormer: a roofed addition to a sloped roof

Emergency egress: emergency escape route (like a window) from a building

Fascia: a flat board used as trim on the face of a cornice

Frieze board: a flat board used as trim where siding meets the soffit of a cornice

Furring strip: a piece of wood, usually 1″ × 2″, used to level walls or ceilings, or to provide a nailing surface

Gable end: the end wall of a building from which the gable of a roof rises

Gable dormer: a dormer with a gable roof

Gable roof: a roof where two sloping sections meet at the peak, forming an "A"

Grout: a mortar or material used to fill gaps in tile work

Gusset: a metal or wooden band used to connect joints in trusses

Gypsum board: drywall, plasterboard, common wallboard

Header: a beam or piece of wood placed over door openings, window openings (and the like) to provide support for the open span

Jack stud: a short stud that usually supports a header

Jack rafter: a rafter that runs from the wall plate to a hip in the roof or from a valley to a ridge

Jamb: the wood casing that holds a door or window

Joist: a wooden member used to support floors and ceilings

Knee wall: a short wall, usually 4' to 5' tall, that extends from the floor to the rafters in an attic

Lally® column: a steel post filled with concrete, used to support load-bearing beams, such as those in a basement

Ledger strip: *See* **Cleat**

Live load: the weight of people, furniture, snow, or other elements that apply weight to a structure (in addition to the structure's deadweight)

Mullion: a vertical member of a window that separates openings in a multiple-opening frame

Muntin: a short member, usually made of wood, that separates the panes of glass in a window

Newel: a post used to begin and end the run of a stair railing

Purlin: a horizontal member responsible for the support of roof rafters

Rafters: boards that are installed between the top plate and the ridge board to support a roof

Ridge board: a board that runs the length of a building, providing support and a nailing surface for rafters

Sheathing: a covering, usually plywood, particleboard, or fibreboard, that's applied to cover rafters and studs

Shed dormer: a dormer with a roof that slopes from the top plate of the dormer back to the main roof

Sleeper system: a system of boards (resting on a concrete floor) that supports a subfloor

Soffit: the underside of a cornice overhang

Stair nose: a part of the stair that extends past the tread and overhangs the stair below

Stair tread: a part of a stairway that provides a surface to step on

Stair winder: a pie-shaped stair tread, used for stairs that turn

Stringer: a support used to hold stair treads

Subfloor: a floor that's nailed to the floor joists and covered with a finished floor

Top plate: a board (or a combination of boards) that forms the top of a wall

Truss: an engineered structure, often made of wood, that serves as a component of a roof system

Appendix

Job Schedule

Phase	Start Date	Completion Date

Material Take-Off

Item	Size	Quantity

Job Budget

Phase	Cost
Plans	
Permits	
Demolition	
Framing	
Stairs	
Dormers	
Plumbing	
Heating	
Electrical	
Insulation	
Drywall	
Paint	
Doors	
Hardware	
Underlayment	
Floor Coverings	
Cabinets	
Counters	
Cleanup	
Other	
Other	
Other	
Other	
Total Cost	

Bid Comparisons

Phase	Vendor	Price

Paint Record

Type of Paint	Supplier	Color	Paint Number

Materials Log

Supplier's Name	
Contact Person	
Order Number	
Date Of Order	
Delivery Date	
Cost Of Order	

Inspection Log

Phase	Ordered	Approved
Rough Plumbing		
Finish Plumbing		
Rough Electrical		
Finish Electrical		
Rough Heating		
Finish Heating		
Framing		
Insulation		
Final		

Punch List

Phase	Okay	Needs Work

Index

D

E

F

H

I

J

W